SELLING YOUR HOUSE

GENERAL REFERENCE

SELLING
YOUR HOUSE

How to manage your agent, find the
best buyer and complete the sale

Adam Walker

How To Books

Cartoons by Mike Flanagan

British Library Cataloguing-in-Publication Data
A catalogue record for this book is available from the British Library.

Published by How To Books Ltd, 3 Newtec Place,
Magdalen Road, Oxford, OX4 1RE, United Kingdom.
Tel: (01865) 793806. Fax: (01865) 248780.
email: info@howtobooks.co.uk
www:howtobooks.co.uk

First edition published 1998
Second impression 1999

Note: The material contained in this book is set out in good faith for
general guidance and no liability can be accepted for loss or expense
incurred as a result of relying in particular circumstances on statements
made in this book. The law and regulations may be complex and liable to
change, and readers should check the current position with the relevant
authorities before making personal arrangements.

Cover design Shireen Nathoo Design
Cover image PhotoDisc
Produced for How To Books by Deer Park Productions.
Typeset by Concept Communications (Design & Print) Ltd, Crayford, Kent.
Printed and bound by Cromwell Press, Trowbridge, Wiltshire.

Contents

List of Illustrations

Preface

A great many 'How to sell your house' books have been published during the last 15 years. Some cover the financial aspects of a move such as raising a mortgage, some cover the legal side of the transaction and some cover how to sell without using an estate agent. However, during the whole of the time that I have been associated with the property market I have never come across a book that explained how to choose and get the best out of an estate agent.

This struck me as very strange. Most house sellers sell through an estate agent and yet there was no such thing as a consumer's guide to estate agency. I felt that there should be and decided to write a book that would answer some of the many questions that I have been asked as a consultant during the last 15 years.

The finished book is in three parts. Chapters 1 to 3 cover how to choose the right estate agent. Ideally this section should be read about eight weeks before the property is put onto the market. Chapters 4 to 7 explain how a good agent should go about finding a buyer. This section should be read as soon as the property is put onto the market. Finally, Chapters 8 to 12 explain some of the common sales progressing problems and give advice on how to overcome them. This section should be used as a reference to dip into as and when a problem occurs.

At the time of writing the Government is in the middle of a comprehensive review of the whole house buying process.

Chapter 13 summarises the proposed changes outlined in the consultation document, *The Key to Easier House Buying and Selling*, published in 1998. In that chapter, I describe some of the potential difficulties as well as benefits, and indicate some of the ways in which you could begin to anticipate the changes.

The proposed legislation will not change the way that houses are marketed and the advice that I have given in the first two sectors of this book is unlikely to change. However, the introduction of such legislation could go a long way towards speeding up the whole process and alleviating many of the problems that I have described in section 3.

This book would not have been possible without the help of a great many people. In particular I should like to thank: Black Horse Agencies, Palmer Snell, the Woolwich Building Society and the Royal Institution of Chartered Surveyors, all of which provided statistical and other information for use in the appendices.

I should also like to thank my secretary Lyn Harding for her patience, good humour and attention to detail during the many drafts of the book.

In this book please read he to mean he or she.

Adam Walker

1
Establishing what the Property is Worth

DOING YOUR OWN RESEARCH

Before you invite an estate agent to value your property you must first establish what it is worth. This may seem like a contradiction in terms but the fact is that estate agents' valuations are often inaccurate. This can happen for a number of reasons:

- **Deliberate overvaluation.** Some estate agents give deliberately over-optimistic valuations because they know that it will help them to get more properties onto their books.

- **Poor research.** An estate agent should have up-to-date knowledge about the prices recently achieved for other properties in the area. Poor research is a very common reason for an inaccurate valuation.

- **Inexperience.** Too many firms of estate agents send staff out on valuation appointments who do not have sufficient experience to value accurately.

- **Local knowledge.** Even an experienced estate agent will not be able to value a property accurately until he has been working in the local area for several months.

The only way to protect yourself against the consequences of an inaccurate valuation is to undertake the most comprehensive price research on your own behalf. In some countries the actual selling price achieved in every property transaction is a matter of public record. In the UK this information often is not publicly available and a degree of subterfuge may be required to obtain the necessary background information.

If you have not already done so, you should consider the idea of registering with some of the local agents as a buyer in order to obtain a selection of sales particulars of properties that are similar to your own. If you really do not want to undertake this type of research, an alternative would be to look through back issues of the local property newspaper to

11

find similar properties (back issues of the local papers are available from the library). The more properties you can find, the more likely it is that your personal valuation will be accurate.

Using the information

The value of a property is determined by two factors: the **prices achieved** for similar properties that have recently been sold, and the **asking prices** of properties that are currently on the market and are competing for the same buyers as your own.

It is relatively easy to establish the value of a house in a road when there are other similar properties. The typical process would be:

Step 1
Research the asking prices of the last five or six properties in the road that have been offered for sale.

Step 2
Ignore properties which were markedly cheaper or more expensive than the others (there is always a reason).

Step 3
Average the price of the remaining properties.

Step 4
Deduct five per cent from the final price to allow for the average difference between the asking and selling prices.

Valuing a more individual property

If you own a more individual property you will need to apply a number of adjustment factors to the comparable properties that are available. Some of the most important factors to take into account are listed below:

Extensions and improvements
You will not generally recover the full cost of extensions and improvements. The proportion of the original cost that is recovered will depend upon the nature of the improvement, for example:

High cost recovery (up to 100 per cent):

● addition of extra bedroom in a style that is in keeping with the original property

● addition of central heating

- redecoration in a neutral style
- addition of a garage

Medium cost recovery (up to 50 per cent)

- addition of ground floor flat roofed extension
- addition of conservatory
- fitted kitchen
- modernisation of bathroom
- loft conversion.

Low cost recovery (less than 25 per cent)

- addition of outdoor swimming pool
- addition of ground floor bathroom
- double glazing
- cavity wall insulation.

Some 'improvements' can substantially reduce the value of the property, for example:

- extensions that occupy the entire garden
- stone cladding
- double glazing on period property
- removal of period features (fireplaces, decorative plasterwork, *etc*).

Repairs
As with improvements, you are unlikely to recover the full cost of repairs that have been made to a property. Most buyers underestimate the cost of repairs and some are prepared to pay a premium for a house in poor condition in order to have the satisfaction of refurbishing it in their own taste.

Area
In many towns a house in one road can command a very substantial premium over houses in the next. It is impossible to generalise about this but the boundaries are usually well-known locally.

Location
A house on a busy road, or one backing onto a railway line will be worth

substantially less than an identical house in a quiet street nearby. An extremely adverse location could reduce the value of a property by up to half.

New developments
Many people will pay a premium to live in a brand new house. All new developments must therefore be excluded from your comparable evidence.

Checking the accuracy of your valuation
You can check the accuracy of your personal valuation by cross referencing it in a number of ways.

How much did you pay?
Your local library will be able to provide you with a table showing the average rise in property values for each year since you purchased your property. Add the appropriate percentage increase to the price which you originally paid for your property. How does it compare with your own valuation?

Current value of properties which you rejected as a purchaser
Before you bought your present property, you will almost certainly have viewed and rejected a number of alternative properties. Check to see if any of these properties, or others that are similar to them, are currently on the market. How does the asking price of each of these properties compare with your own valuation?

Remortgage valuations
If you have remortgaged your house at any time, try adding the average percentage rise in property values since the remortgage to the surveyor's valuation. How does this figure compare with your own valuation?

Friends and acquaintances who have recently bought and sold
People are strangely reticent about revealing the price that they paid or obtained for their property but there is no harm in asking. People often tell their neighbours that they paid more or less for their property than they really did. You should therefore treat all information obtained in this way with the greatest suspicion, particularly information which is passed on by a third party.

   Once you have done everything possible to research and check the accuracy of your personal valuation you are ready to begin to prepare for the estate agents' valuation appointments.

PREPARING YOUR PROPERTY FOR SALE

Presentation is vital

The maxim 'presentation is vital' was never more true than when selling a house. It is therefore extremely important to carry out any necessary cosmetic work before you put your property on the market.

House buyers form their impressions very quickly – indeed research shows that half of all buyers make the final decision before they even get inside the font door! If such a high proportion of buyers are going to make their decision from outside then this is where you too must start.

Checking the outside

Go and stand in the street at least 100 yards away from your property. Take a good hard look and try to see it through the eyes of someone who has never seen it before. What do you see? Have the neighbours' houses been decorated more recently than yours? If so consider redecorating at least the front elevation.

Move slowly forwards, ten yards at a time. What do you see as you move closer? Could your teenage son be persuaded to park his battered old car somewhere else for a few weeks? Are any tiles missing from the roof? Does the hedge need trimming? Is the font fence in good condition? Does the front garden need tidying?

Enter the front garden. Does the gate operate smoothly? Is the front door in good decorative condition? Are there cobwebs in the porch? Does the door bell work?

Open the front door and step inside. Take a long critical look at the entrance hall. Bear in mind that it is the first room that potential purchasers will see and consider whether any work is necessary to brighten it up. Before you leave the entrance hall think carefully about what order the rooms in the house should be shown in. It is important to ensure that buyers see the most attractive rooms first.

Checking the inside

Go round the house in the order that purchasers will see it and check each room thoroughly. In particular look for the following:

● Does any room need redecorating?

● Are there any stains or damp patches?

● Are there any cracks?

● Do the carpets need cleaning?

- Do any light bulbs need replacing?

- Are any windows overshadowed by trees or foliage?

- Are the windows dirty?

- Is the garden tidy?

- Are the fences in good order?

Decorating to sell
If any room does need redecorating it is best to stick to light neutral colours which will make the room look bigger and lighter. Save expressing your individualism for your next house.

More extensive works
Generally speaking it is not worth undertaking more major works in order to facilitate a sale. If you are thinking of undertaking repair work, you should bear in mind that most purchasers tend to underestimate the true cost of repairs so you are likely to be better off leaving them as they are. If you are thinking of undertaking cosmetic work you should bear in mind that most buyers would prefer to buy a cheaper property and install their own choice of kitchen, bathroom or carpets, *etc.*

Finishing touches
In addition to the above you might also consider:

- **Net curtains** block out a great deal of natural light and can also make rooms look smaller. Consider taking them down while the house is on the market.

- Rooms can be made to seem very dark by heavy **curtains** which cannot be drawn back off the windows. Consider tying such curtains back while the house is on the market.

- Large pieces of **furniture** will make rooms seem smaller. Consider repositioning or even storing such items while the house is on the market.

- A hanging basket in the porch or fresh **flowers** in the entrance hall can make a real difference to a buyer's first impression of your house.

When considering all of the above, bear in mind the golden rule that 'the sooner they see it the more important it is'. A dingy entrance hall could be extremely off-putting; your daughter's fluorescent purple bedroom will have less effect on a potential purchaser's decision.

Organising a trial viewing

Once you have attended to all the necessary jobs, ask a friend to 'view' your property. Ask them to point out anything that you have missed. Ask them also for their honest opinion on one very important matter: **How does your house smell**? I am not joking. Despite the fact that smell is one of our most powerful senses, many people do not realise that the human nose is only programmed to detect new smells. To you Fido stopped 'smelling' when he was a 12-week-old puppy. To strangers he could now smell strongly enough to prevent a sale for months! Even the bravest estate agent will not tell you this - find a friend who will.

Consider paying for a surveyor's report

Very few people consider instructing a surveyor to look at a house that they are selling, but a **survey report** can be a valuable marketing tool. Many buyers are nervous about making an offer for a house for fear that problems will later be revealed on survey. If this does happen, the cost to them could be several hundred pounds in abortive legal and survey fees and two to three weeks' wasted time.

A survey report is not transferable and a buyer would have no legal comeback on the surveyor if the report was later found to be inaccurate. However, the availability of a survey report can do a great deal to allay a buyer's fears and it could prove to be well worth its cost. A survey report is particularly valuable if you are selling a house that is large, old or in poor condition.

CASE STUDY

Being blinded by the highest valuation

John and Sarah asked three agents to value their property, a traditional three-bedroom semi in a road of 100 similar houses. Agent A valued it at £70,000, agent B at £72,000 and agent C at £80,000. John and Sarah instructed agent C at an asking price of £79,950 and signed a 20 week sole agency contract.

After four weeks no one had viewed the property so John rang the agent to ask why. The agent said that he thought that the price was too high and advised a reduction. When John reminded the agent that he had said it was worth £80,000 the agent replied, 'valuation is not an exact science, a property is only worth what someone is prepared to pay for it'.

John said that if that was the case he would withdraw his property and give it to agent A whose original valuation had been more accurate. The agent replied that if he did this he would sue John and Sarah for breaking their 20 week sole agency contract. Faced with no other alternative John and Sarah reduced the asking price of their property and agent C sold it shortly afterwards for £70,000.

With hindsight John and Sarah wished that they had instructed agent A or B.

CHECKLIST

● Do you have a rough idea of what your property is worth? Is this based on other properties that are for sale and sold in the area?

● Have you made a proper allowance for the condition of your property and for the value of any improvements and extensions?

● Does your property look at its very best?

● Have you asked a close friend to conduct a viewing?

2
Choosing an Estate Agent

DECIDING WHETHER YOU NEED AN ESTATE AGENT

More than three-quarters of all house sellers in England and Wales use an estate agent. They do so because they believe that, even after allowing for commission, an agent will achieve a higher price for their property than they could achieve themselves. They are usually right.

Why will an estate agent achieve a higher price?

The price that is achieved for a property is determined, largely, by the law of supply and demand. If a property is exposed to a greater number of potential buyers, it will usually sell for a higher price.

One of the most important functions of an estate agent is, therefore, to act as an efficient net to catch every potential house buyer in the price range. When it comes to finding potential buyers, an estate agent has four important advantages over the private seller. They are:

- newspaper advertising

- high street premises

- presence in *Yellow Pages*

- For Sale boards.

Newspaper advertising
An estate agent will run prominent advertisements in the local newspapers each week. The number of enquiries generated is related very closely to the size of the advertisement. A small private advertisement would do well to generate half a dozen enquiries. The estate agent's full page advertisement will generate many times this many.

A second point to consider regarding advertising is that many potential purchasers, particularly those from out of the area, buy a local newspaper only once. Having registered with all the local agents, they then wait to be contacted with details of suitable properties. By advertising for only one week the private vendor will reach only a fraction of these buyers.

High street premises
Many buyers like to register by calling into the estate agent's office in person. Out-of-town buyers in particular tend to find 'estate agents' row' and register with all the agents in it. The lack of high street premises will further reduce the number of potential purchasers that the private vendor is able to attract.

Yellow Pages
Many buyers register with agents by working through *Yellow Pages*. The lack of an entry here will further hamper the private vendor.

For Sale boards
The typical estate agent will have several dozen For Sale boards up at any one time. Each one of these boards will attract several new buyers and cumulatively they will be responsible for attracting around a quarter of all buyers. The private vendor with just his own single For Sale will fail to attract most of these purchasers.

Given all these advantages, an estate agent should be able to attract many times more purchasers for a property than a private vendor. Consequently, even a bad agent will usually be able to achieve a better price for your property than you could yourself.

Other benefits of using an agent
In addition to finding the maximum number of potential purchasers, a good estate agent will be able to help with your sale in several other important ways. These include:

- **Valuation advice**. A good agent will give advice on the value of your property and help you to decide on the optimum asking price.

- **Marketing**. A good agent will play an active role in persuading potential purchasers to view your property.

- **Security**. A good agent will check out potential viewers to ensure that they are genuine.

- **Negotiation**. A good agent will use his negotiation skills to obtain the highest possible price.

- **Qualification**. A good agent will check out your prospective buyers to ensure that they are actually in a position to proceed with the transaction.

- **Supervision**. A good agent will keep a close eye on your sale and help to resolve any problems that arise prior to completion.

It is certainly possible to sell a house privately but there is no doubt that a good agent will earn his fee many times over. I would urge you to use one.

FINDING THE RIGHT ESTATE AGENT

In most large towns there is a bewildering selection of estate agents to choose from. To the casual observer they might appear to be all very much the same. On closer examination you will find that they most certainly are not. The best agent in the town might be able to achieve thousands of pounds more for your property than his least effective competitor. With this sort of money at stake it is worth going to considerable trouble to choose the right agent for the job.

The tell-tale signs that differentiate an outstanding agent from an average one can be grouped under two categories: the 'marketing campaign' and the 'service standards'.

The marketing campaign

The number of potential purchasers that each agent has on his books will be governed by the effectiveness of his marketing campaign. The most effective agent could have three or four times more buyers in his register than his least effective competitor and this gives him a much better chance of achieving a premium price for your property. The effectiveness of each agent's marketing campaign can be judged by looking at the three key areas of advertising, board presence and office position.

Newspaper advertising

Newspaper advertising is the single most important source of potential purchasers and it is, therefore, worth taking some trouble to assess each agent's effectiveness in this area. Collect together all the local newspapers for a three to four week period and look for the following features:

- **Size**. The leading agents will nearly always have the largest advertisements. There is a direct correlation between the size of the advertisement and the number of enquiries generated.

- **Choice of publication**. Advertising costs vary widely between different newspapers and, generally speaking, advertisers get what they pay for. If in doubt you might consider phoning the local newspapers to enquire about advertising rates and circulation figures so that you can make your own assessment of which agent has the highest local advertising budget.

- **Position**. Certain pages in a newspaper generate far more enquiries than others. Generally speaking:

  - the nearer the front the better

  - right hand pages are better than left hand pages

  - the front cover, back cover and centre pages usually get a good response.

  The leading agents usually book the prime positions on a long term contract. You should be cautious about using an agent who has a consistently poor position.

- **Frequency**. The leading agents will advertise every week throughout the year (with the possible exception of December). You should be cautious about using an agent who advertises only sporadically.

- **Layout**. The advertisement should be easy to read with an attractive layout and plenty of space between the properties. Advertisements that cram too many properties into a small space generate fewer enquiries.

- **Colour**. Full colour advertisements generate far more enquiries than black and white ones. If only two or three agents are advertising in colour, they will have a considerable advantage over their competitors.

- **Variety**. Beware of the agent who advertises the same houses every week – he may be having trouble attracting new instructions (and there is usually a reason for this).

- **Content**. What sort of properties are advertised by each agent? Are they cheaper or more expensive than your own? There is no point putting an ordinary house with an up-market agent or vice versa.

Board presence

Estate agents' boards are another very important source of enquiries. Do a rough count of which agents have the largest number of boards up in your area. It is likely that each of these boards will have already generated several enquiries from potential purchasers for your property. Pay particular attention to Sold boards. The agent who has recently sold several houses in your road could well be the best agent to handle the sale of your house.

Office position

A large percentage of potential purchasers like to register their requirements in person. The position and prominence of an estate agent's office is often, therefore, an important factor. The prominent high street office will usually register several times as many potential purchasers as its small backstreet competitor.

Standards of customer service

Before you rush off to instruct the agent with the biggest advertisement and the most prominent office, you should pause to consider that registering the largest number of potential purchasers is not an automatic guarantee of success. In order to sell houses effectively, an agent needs to persuade potential purchasers to view the properties that they have for sale. It is here that so many agents fall down.

There is only one way to establish which of the local agents offers the best standard of service and that is to register with them all as a buyer. If you are moving locally you can register as a genuine purchaser. If you are not buying locally you could register as a purchaser for a property that is similar to the one which you wish to sell, perhaps saying that your present property is rented. You will find that the level of service which you receive as a purchaser varies enormously between agents. The signs of an effective agent are:

- **Initial response**. The telephone should be answered promptly and cheerfully.

- **Rapport**. The agent should work hard to build a rapport rather than just reading questions off a list.

- **Qualification**. The agent should establish quickly whether you are in a position to buy immediately or whether you have a property yet to sell. This will enable him to work more effectively by spending more time with his best prospects.

- **Sales effort**. The agent should describe a couple of suitable properties over the phone and ask you for an immediate commitment to view them. This is far more effective than just passively sending out details.

- **Property details**. An accurately chosen selection of property details should arrive by post the next working day. Some firms might even deliver details by hand to local purchasers. The details should be attractively presented, preferably with full colour photographs.

- **Telephone follow-up**. The effective agent will telephone you approximately 24 hours after you have received the details and make another attempt to get a viewing appointment. Purchasers who are followed up by telephone are far more likely to view than those who are left to contact the agent themselves.

- **Ongoing follow-up**. The effective agent will continue to telephone you at least once a week to try to persuade you to view properties that are new to the market.

- **Persistence**. To be effective an agent must be persistent. You need someone who will really *sell* your property, not just wait for someone to buy it. However, the effective agent should know when to give up gracefully and should never become over-aggressive.

You will usually find that the service given by one or two agents stands head and shoulders above the service given by the rest. These agents should definitely be included on your short list.

Owning up

It is unlikely that you will ever need to own up to your subterfuge. You can tell the agents that did not measure up that you have now found a property to buy. The agents that you do choose to invite to value your property will often not notice that someone on their applicant register has asked for a valuation appointment. If they do, you can simply admit that you wanted to test their service before instructing them. They will probably be quite flattered to have been chosen by such an objective process.

How not to choose an estate agent

As a home owner you are likely to receive regular approaches from agents who are touting for business. These will come in a number of formats:

The printed leaflet

A typical message would be 'Now is the time to sell. Call Bloggs estate agents for a free valuation without obligation'. Many estate agents deliver tens of thousands of such leaflets every year. The fact that you have received one does not mean that the company who sent it will be any better able to sell your house than the others.

The photocopied letter

A typical message would be 'Dear Householder, We have just sold a house in your road and urgently need similar properties in the area'. This type of letter deserves to be taken a little more seriously. The agent would not have chosen your road if he did not have a demand for houses in it. However, if you do respond to such an approach you should ask the agent to prove that he really has sold a property and that he has other buyers available for similar properties in the area.

The individually addressed letter

The format of this letter will be similar to the photocopied letter described above and it should be dealt with in a similar way. The fact that it is addressed to you by name means only that the agent has looked up your name on the electoral register, which is available in the public library.

Although it may sometimes be worth responding to a touting letter, you should not allow the receipt of one to influence unduly your choice of agent. You are far more likely to find the right agent to market your property by objective research than by responding to a cleverly written letter.

Selecting the final short list

Having finished your study of all the local agents you will be in a position to compile a short list of agents that you wish to see. Sometimes one agent will win hands down in every category, but more often than not you will be forced to compromise. Perhaps the agent with the biggest advertisement and the most prominent office gave you very poor services as a buyer. This could be a business in decline. Perhaps the dynamic manager who built the office up has recently been replaced by someone of a lower calibre. Whatever the reason, such a company is best avoided. At the other end of the scale you may have received outstanding service from an agent with a backstreet office and sporadic advertising. Again you should be cautious. Service is important but it cannot make up for a lack of potential buyers to sell to.

The safest choice would be to confine your list to companies who score reasonably well in both the key areas of effective marketing and effective customer service. On this basis you should select three or four agents to value your property.

ARRANGING THE VALUATION APPOINTMENT

Being prepared to answer questions

When you telephone to arrange a valuation appointment, the agent will want to ask you a number of questions. Beware. It is probably not in your best interest to answer them all at this time. The likely questions can be divided into three categories.

Questions about the property
The agent will ask for a detailed description of your property. He needs this information in order to research its value prior to his visit. You should describe your property accurately and thoroughly, paying particular attention to any unusual features such as an extension.

Questions about you
The agent will also ask for a lot of background information about you. He will want to know the reason for your move, your anticipated time-scale and whether you have already contacted other agents. The agent's purpose in asking such questions is to ascertain whether you are serious about moving or whether you just want a valuation. Your answers to these questions will determine how seriously your enquiry is taken and also, very often, the seniority of the member of staff sent out to see you. For this reason these questions must be answered with some care. In particular:

● Never admit to being in a hurry to sell. This could mean a lower valuation.

● Always say that you will be inviting several agents around before deciding who to instruct on a sole agency basis (a more senior member of staff will often be sent to sell the firm's service against competition).

Questions about the property's value
Some agents will ask you what price you are hoping to achieve for your

property over the telephone. If you reveal this at this stage there is a real danger that the agent will tell you the price that you want to hear instead of giving you a properly researched valuation. You should therefore decline to answer this question at this time. Say something like 'I do have a price in mind but I should like to hear your opinion first'.

Having answered the agent's questions, the next thing to do is to agree on a time for the appointment. Your valuation appointment is an extremely important occasion, and it is my belief that it is an occasion where two heads are better than one. If you have a partner, then both of you should be present. If not you might consider asking a trusted friend to sit through each appointment with you.

The amount of time each agent will wish to spend with you will vary widely but, to be on the safe side, one and a half hours should be allowed between appointments. It is embarrassing for everyone if the next agent arrives before the previous one has left. The best time for an appointment is undoubtedly a weekday when most agents will have more time to explain their service fully. On no account should an agent be invited to undertake a valuation after dark. Artificial light makes a property look so different that accurate valuation is impossible.

Finally, do not be frightened to stand firm on your preferred appointment times. Agents often try to sound busier than they are in order to impress potential clients and may be able to move 'another appointment' if you insist on a particular time.

MEETING YOUR ESTATE AGENT

Background and first impressions

Estate agency is a profession full of eccentrics. It is therefore important to resist the temptation to judge each agent on the basis of first impressions alone. The dishevelled-looking chap who arrives by bicycle, ten minutes late for the appointment, could very easily be the best agent for the job.

After exchanging pleasantries, the agent will probably want to sit down with you to discuss the background to your move. During this part of the appointment the agent will be trying to establish three things:

1. How serious are you about moving?

2. What is your time-scale?

3. Why are you moving?

Thinking about your answers

The experienced estate agent will make this stage of the appointment seem like nothing more than an informal exchange of pleasantries but in fact every single question will have a purpose. For example the purpose of a question like 'are you moving with work?' might be to find out if your company will be paying the fees so that a higher than usual commission rate may be quoted. Your answers to all such questions should reassure the agent that you are serious about moving. However, you must at the same time be very careful not to say anything that may later prejudice your negotiating position. If, for example, you are desperate to sell your property quickly, you should keep this to yourself, at very least until an asking price and a commission level have been agreed and preferably until the property has been on the market for a couple of weeks. If you do not, you may find that you are quoted a lower asking price, an increased commission level, or both!

Having established the background to your move, the agent will look round the property. I recommend that he should be allowed to do so alone. During this initial inspection tour the agent will value your property by comparing it with all the others that he has seen. This process requires great concentration and the valuation will probably be more accurate if the agent is not obliged to make small talk during his inspection.

On his return the agent should be ready to discuss his valuation with you. I say 'should' because just occasionally you will come across an agent who is unwilling to discuss his valuation without first discussing it with his colleagues back at the office. If the property is very large or unusual then there is some justification for this. If it is not you should ask the agent bluntly why he feels unable to give you a valuation on the spot. The most likely reasons are inexperience or lack of preparation. If you suspect that either is the case you should find another agent.

AGREEING AN ASKING PRICE

Beware of the agent who overvalues

The worst possible way to choose an estate agent is to instruct the one that quotes the highest asking price. Unfortunately this is exactly how many home owners make their decision. A minority of estate agents exploit this by deliberately overvaluing the properties that they see in order to get instructions. Once instructed, they will try to persuade the client to reduce the asking price in the hope that the property can still be sold before the end of the sole agency period. Such agents should be avoided like the plague. Fortunately they are very easy to spot.

An agent who deliberately overvalues will spend the whole valuation appointment trying to find out the price that you want to hear. The least subtle will ask you directly for the price that you are hoping to achieve. Most will try to find out by more subtle methods.

One common method is to ask you how long you have owned the house and how much you originally paid for it. By applying the appropriate annual adjustment factors the agent will be able to calculate the likely present value. An alternative method is to ask how much you are intending to spend on your next house and then later on by how much you are planning to increase your present mortgage. Some very simple mathematics will give the agent the price that you are hoping to achieve for your present house. A more subtle technique involves the agent mentioning the prices of a number of other houses that have been sold recently. Each time a price is mentioned the agent will watch closely for your reaction. Each time you look disappointed, he will raise his 'valuation' for your property until he is sure that you will be happy with the figure that he gives you.

You have absolutely nothing to gain from revealing your assessment of the property's value before you have heard the agent's opinion and my advice would be to respond to all such questions by saying something like 'I really would like to hear your valuation before I discuss my expectations with you'. Faced with this response the agent will have no choice but to give his own opinion of value.

Control your reaction

However disappointed you are by the agent's figure, it is important not to show it at this stage. In order to obtain the maximum benefit from the agent's experience, you must first work calmly through four further stages:

Stage 1: Confirmation

Some agents try to leave themselves room for manoeuvre by saying that the property is worth between £50-£55,000. It is important to try to pin the agent down to a precise figure. Try asking him in what circumstances he would expect to achieve both the lower and the higher figure.

Stage 2: Qualification

The main purpose of this stage is to prevent an agent from trying to wriggle out of his original valuation when challenged. He may try to do this using words such as:

● My original figure of £65,000 is the price I expect to obtain after negotiation. The asking price of course would be much higher.

To avoid this you should ask the agent to confirm every aspect of his valuation by asking questions such as:

● What would be your recommended asking price?

● What price would you expect to obtain after negotiation?

● How long would you expect it to take to find a buyer at this price?

Stage 3. Justification
Ask the agent to explain to you the exact process by which he arrived at his valuation. In particular ask him which comparable properties he took into account before arriving at his final figure. A good agent should be able to justify his valuation without hesitation, by referring to at least three comparable properties. A really good agent will have brought the sales particulars of all comparable properties with him to the appointment.

Stage 4. Negotiation
Once you have heard both the agent's valuation and his justification for it, you can safely reveal your own expectation and how you arrived at it. The process of negotiation which is likely to follow is probably best demonstrated by the use of some fictitious case studies.

CASE STUDIES

Undervaluation – vendor concedes
Agent's initial valuation £90,000: recommended asking price £93,950.

Vendor: I'm sorry to tell you that your valuation is £5,000 less than I was hoping to achieve and I'd like to tell you how I arrived at my figure. I have two justifications:

(1) The property opposite which is identical to mine was sold eight weeks ago for £96,000.

(2) I believe that number 86, which has no garage, was sold last month for £89,000.

On this evidence I really do expect to get £95,000 for mine.

Agent: The original price agreed for the house opposite was indeed

£96,000 but the building society valuer downvalued it on survey to £90,000 and that is what it sold for. I therefore stand by my valuation of £90,000.

Vendor: But also number 89 sold for £89,950 and it doesn't have a garage.

Agent: When number 89 was sold the house opposite was for sale at £99,950. This made 89 seem good value. Now that it is known that the house opposite sold for £90,000 this sets a ceiling on the price achievable in the road.

Vendor: I accept your argument but I would like to quote an initial asking price of £96,950 not £93,950.

Agent: I believe that the price would discourage potential viewers.

Vendor: All right, then £95,950.

Agent: I will try it at that figure for 14 days but we must review the price after that.

Undervaluation – agent concedes
Agent's initial valuation £65,000: recommended asking price £66,950.

Vendor: I am disappointed by your figure. Number 12 sold at £69,000 and number 19 is for sale at £69,950.

Agent: We sold a house in the next road a few weeks ago for £65,000. I believe my valuation is correct.

Vendor: You didn't refer to number 12 or to number 19 when citing your comparable evidence. I have to ask whether you took them into account in your valuation.

Agent: We didn't handle those sales.

Vendor: That doesn't answer my question.

Agent: I have based my valuation on the house which we sold in the next road.

Vendor: In view of the price achieved for number 12, I should like to quote £69,950 for my property. Would you be prepared to take it on at that figure?

Agent: Yes.

Vendor: Very well. If I instruct you it will be at £69,950.

Overvaluation – agent concedes

Agent's initial valuation £45,000: recommended asking price £46,750.

Vendor: My own valuation was £3,000 less than yours. I based it on two other identical flats in the block, numbers 4 and 22, both of which have sold for £42,000 within the last three months. Could you explain to me again how you arrived at your figure?

Agent: The even numbered flats are at the front of the block. They always seem to sell for less.

Vendor: That wasn't true when I bought this flat. What has changed since?

Agent: I don't know, but it is generally true.

Vendor: When did you last sell a flat in this block?

Agent: I've been in the agency for five years. The company must have sold loads.

Vendor: How about you personally?

Agent: Well – I only moved to this branch a couple of months ago.

Vendor: While I would like to get £45,000 I don't believe that I can do it in the time available. If I instruct you it will be at a lower figure, but thank you for your advice.

The final decision

Always remember that the final decision on an asking price is yours and yours alone. There is absolutely nothing to stop you instructing an agent at an asking price that is different from the one recommended. The agent's job is to advise, your job is to weigh up advice from as many different sources as possible and to decide. No one else should make that decision for you.

Assessing the agent's sales presentation

Giving an accurate valuation is one thing, achieving that price is quite another. Your decision as to which agent to instruct cannot therefore be made on the basis of the valuation alone.

Once an asking price has been agreed, the estate agent should, of his own accord, tell you more about the service that his company offers. It is best to leave the agent to highlight the key features of his service but if necessary you should prompt him in order to ensure that the following areas are covered:

1. Experience:

● How long has he personally been in the business?

● How long has he worked in the local area?

● How long has he worked for his present employer?

● How experienced are the other members of his team?

2. Company background:

● Who owns the business?

● How long has the firm been established?

3. Advertising:

● Where does the firm advertise?

● Do the advertisements have any special features (*eg* colour photographs)?

4. Property particulars:

● Does the company use colour photographs on its particulars?

5. Coverage:

● Does the company have offices in other local towns?

● If so, will your property details be available there?

6. Opening hours:

● What are the usual opening hours?

● Is the office staffed by full-time people at weekends?

7. Sales methods:

● Are buyers usually contacted by telephone or by post?

● Will the agent accompany viewings or will you be left to show buyers round yourself?

8. Qualification/security:

● How does the agency check to ensure that buyers are genuine?

● How will they check that buyers can afford to buy your property before arranging an appointment?

9. Sales progressing:

● What action will the agent take to ensure that your sale reaches a satisfactory conclusion?

10. Recent results:

● Has the agent recently sold other properties in your area?

● How many houses do they usually sell each month? (They might not tell you but there is no harm in asking.)

11. Testimonials:

● Can your agent show you testimonials from satisfied clients?

By the end of this part of the interview you will probably have a very good idea about whether you wish to instruct the agent or not. The final factor in your decision will be the commission level.

NEGOTIATING THE FEE

The maxim 'you get what you pay for' is true for most things in life and estate agency is no exception. If you are quoted an unexpectedly low fee the first thing to do is to check that you are being quoted for a full estate agency service. You will very often find that the lower fee is in fact being quoted by a property shop or by an agent who operates on an exclusive agency basis.

Property shops v conventional estate agents

Property shops charge much lower fees than estate agents. They are able to do this because they charge their fee at the point of instruction and keep it regardless of whether a sale is achieved or not. The inherent disadvantage of paying an up-front fee is that the property shop has no financial incentive to sell your house. It is probably because of this that the success rate of most property shops is lower than that of most estate agents. Taking everything into account a conventional estate agent is usually likely to offer better value for money.

Responding to a lower than expected fee

If you are quoted a low fee by a conventional estate agent, you must establish how he is able to undercut his competitors. You might say something like 'The fee that you have quoted is half a per cent less than your main competitors. Could I ask how you are able to offer the same service at a lower price?'

On closer examination you will often find that the lower fee is financed by less advertising, fewer staff, cheaper premises or some other such economy. If this is the case you should weigh up very carefully how these economies might affect the agent's ability to achieve the best price for your property.

Responding to a higher than expected fee

If you are quoted a fee that is higher than expected, you should challenge it firmly but politely. You might say something like 'I am impressed by your service but your fee is half a per cent more than I've been quoted elsewhere. How can you justify this differential?' Faced with such a challenge the effective agent might try one of two approaches:

1. He might try to justify the differential by pointing out further features of his service which are not offered by his competitors, *eg* colour advertising or longer opening hours.

2. He might argue that the same negotiation techniques which enable him to obtain premium fee levels from his clients will also enable him to achieve a premium price for your property!

Both arguments have some merit. It is for you to decide whether you believe that superior marketing or superior negotiation techniques will indeed lead to a higher sale price, but my experience is that they often do.

The less effective agent will respond to his fee level being challenged in one of two other ways:

1.   He will immediately match the lower fee. If he does this you must ask whether he would give in so easily when negotiating an offer for your property with a potential purchaser.

2.   He will suggest that the extra commission is added on to your asking price. This is quite indefensible. If the property is really worth more why did the agent not say so sooner? If it is not then you will end up paying his whole fee anyway.

Some non-conventional fee arrangements

Most agents express their fee as a percentage of the selling price but there is no need for the fee to be calculated in this way. The following alternatives may be appropriate in different circumstances. Their introduction may also often help to resolve fee negotiations that have become deadlocked.

The split percentage fee

Most of an agent's skill is used to persuade a purchaser to increase his offer by the last few thousand pounds. This arrangement recognises this by giving an agent a much higher reward if he achieves a premium price. A split fee arrangement works like this:

● Conventional fee

Asking price	£109,950
Expected sales price	£100,000
Fee payable £100,000 x 2%	£2,000

● Split fee

Asking price	£109,950	
Fee agreement	1.5% of the first £95,000 and 10% of any balance achieved above this figure	
Price achieved	£105,000	
Fee payable	£95,000 x 1.5% =	£1,425
+	£10,000 x 10% =	£1,000
Total fee payable		£2,425

In this example the agent is £425 better off, but the vendor is £4,265 better off!

This sort of arrangement gives the agent a tremendous incentive to achieve a premium price and can be an excellent arrangement for both parties.

The fixed fee

It is agreed that a fee of £X will be paid regardless of the price achieved for the property. This arrangement would most commonly be used for very expensive properties, or at the agent's instigation, for a very cheap property (*eg* a mobile home) where he wishes to charge a minimum fee but is embarrassed to quote this as 10 per cent of the selling price. Fixed fees have their place but the drawback is that the agent has no financial incentive to achieve a higher price for the vendor.

The part up-front fee

An agent knows that he will only sell approximately 50 per cent of all the houses that he takes on. The remainder will be withdrawn by vendors who decide not to sell after all or will be sold by another agent. The cost of marketing properties that are not sold is considerable and ultimately this cost has to be recovered from clients who do sell. For this reason agents are often prepared to make a substantial reduction in their commission in return for a relatively small non-refundable advance payment.

For example:

Usual fee 2%, selling price of £100,000: fee = £2,000
Alternative £500 advance payment
1% fee payable on sale
Total fee payable £1,500
Saving to client £500.

This method is only to be recommended if you are absolutely sure that you want to sell your property and if you are also certain about your choice of agent.

The personal bonus

By arrangement with the office manager, you may be able to agree to pay a personal bonus to the individual negotiator who sells your property. This arrangement is particularly appropriate if you need to sell your property quickly. Increasing the agent's commission from 2 to 2.5 per cent would have little effect on the way that the agent marketed your property. Offering a 0.5 per cent bonus to the individual negotiator who sells the property could do a great deal to ensure that your property is given priority.

I would stress that such arrangements should only be made with the full knowledge and approval of the manager and/or the proprietor. You must also make it clear to the negotiator who receives the bonus that he or she will be responsible for paying income tax on the monies paid.

After considering every possible alternative fee structure and engaging in five or ten minutes of lively negotiation you will be almost ready to make your final choice of agent.

MAKING YOUR FINAL DECISION

At the end of the valuation appointment, the agent will probably ask you to make a decision on the spot. You should not do so for several reasons. Firstly, however good the first agent is, the next one might be even better. Having taken the trouble to compile a short list, you really should see everyone on it. Secondly, by delaying your decision for a couple of days you will get one last opportunity to test each agent's qualities of persistence and determination by seeing how vigorously they follow the appointment up.

Thirdly, a number if important decisions have yet to be made about the terms and duration of the agency agreement. Such decisions are best not made under pressure.

Testing the agent's persistence

At the end of the appointment thank the agent for his advice and say politely but firmly that you will be making a final decision within a few days. Most agents will accept this without further argument. The really effective agent, however, will not take no for an answer so easily and may try several more times to get a decision from you on the spot. This is an occasion when determination and persistence should be admired. The agent who tries hard to win your instructions is likely to be equally persistent when persuading potential purchasers to view your house.

The really skilled agent will seem to have an answer for every objection that you raise, for example:

Customer:	I'd like to think it over.
Agent:	Of course, but exactly what do you need to think about before deciding?
Customer:	I've got one more agent to see.

Agent: Of course, but exactly what are you hoping they will offer which I don't?

It can be surprisingly difficult to resist a determined onslaught from a really good sales person but resist you must. You cannot be sure of making the right decision under such pressure. The best way to counter such sales techniques is to keep repeating calmly but firmly that you will not make such an important decision on the spot.

Once the final agent has left, you are at least in a position to make your final decision. Often one agent will come out head and shoulders above the others. If this is not the case, it may be helpful to compare the best two or three agents using the comparison table at the end of Chapter 3.

CASE STUDY

Alan and Mary are tempted by a low commission

Alan and Mary asked three estate agents to value their property. All recommended quite similar asking prices so the decision came down to service and fee alone. Agent A quoted 1 per cent, agent B quoted 1.5 per cent and agent C 2 per cent. Alan and Mary had some reservations about agent A. His office was in a back street, his advertising was sporadic and he did not have many boards up in their area. Nevertheless as he offered a saving on commission of £700 they decided to give him a go and signed a four week sole agency agreement.

After four weeks nothing much had happened, only two people had viewed the property and neither of them was in a position to proceed.

At this point John and Mary disinstructed agent A and instructed agent C. Agent C had just sold another house in the street and had several interested applicants on his books. Seven viewings were arranged during the first week and the sale was agreed the following Monday.

Commenting on their experience Mary said, 'it's clear now that agent C was far better equipped to find a buyer for our property and they were worth the extra fee. Agent A just didn't have enough buyers. Thank goodness we only signed a four week agency agreement.'

CHECKLIST

● Have you checked out where your intended agent advertises and how his advertisement compares with the other agents in the town?

● Does the agent that you intend to use have a good number of For Sale and Sold boards up in your area?

- Do you know where each agent's office is? Does your intended agent trade from a busy position?

- Have you registered with your intended agent as a 'purchaser' to test the service that they give?

- Have you arranged the valuation appointment for a time when both you and your partner can be present?

- Was your intended agent able to *prove* that their recommended asking price was realistic?

- Have you considered alternative fee arrangements to the conventional straight percentage?

- Are you sure that your final choice has been made on the basis of value for money rather than on price alone?

3
Exploring Agency Terms

COMMON AGENCY TERMS

Southern England

There are four types of agency agreement in use in Southern England:

Sole agency
This means that just one agent is instructed to market a property. It is common these days for agents to ask for a minimum period of sole agency – an initial period of eight to twelve weeks would be typical. If you choose to instruct an agent on a sole agency basis, you will probably be asked to sign a sole agency agreement. You should be aware that this is a legally binding contract which will prevent you from instructing any other agent during the sole agency period. If you break the agreement you may be liable to pay two lots of estate agents' commission, one to the original sole agent and one to the selling agent.

Joint sole agency
This means that two agents agree to share the agency commission regardless of which one of them achieves a sale. The most common circumstance for a joint sole agency agreement is where an expensive or unusual property needs to be marketed by a London agent in addition to a local one. Fee levels for joint sole agency are significantly higher than for a conventional sole agency.

Multiple agency
This means that one or more agents are instructed to sell a property on the basis that whichever achieves a sale keeps the entire fee. Multiple agency is a very combative and inefficient way of doing business and because of this some agents will not accept instructions at all on this basis.

Sole selling rights
This works on a similar basis to sole agency. The difference is that the agent is entitled to receive a fee if the property is sold within the agency

period *even if the agent was not responsible for achieving the sale*. If you sold your house to your brother, a fee would still technically be payable. There is no justification for any agent to ask for sole selling rights and you should not agree to instruct anyone on this basis. Thankfully the use of sole selling rights agreements is now extremely rare.

Northern England

The agency system in Northern England (defined as approximately north of Birmingham) operates in a different way. The four types of agency agreement detailed above are all available, but in Northern England multiple agency agreements are much rarer. A second difference is that two types of sole agency agreement are in use:

Inclusive agency
This is the standard southern sole agency system where a fee is payable only if the property is sold.

Exclusive agency
This means that you will be liable to pay the agent's out-of-pocket expenses in addition to sales commission. These expenses will include items such as advertising, photography and the cost of erecting a For Sale board. You will be liable to pay the agent's expenses *whether or not the property is sold*. You may also be liable to pay a withdrawal fee if the property is withdrawn from the market for any reason.

CHOOSING THE MOST APPROPRIATE TYPE OF AGENCY AGREEMENT

Southern England
Circumstances where a sole agency is appropriate
Sole agency has four important advantages over a multiple agency agreement:

● **It is cheaper.** Because a sole agent has a greater chance of receiving a fee he can afford to charge a lower rate of commission. Sole agency fees are typically 20-50 per cent lower than multiple agency rates.

● **You will usually get a better service.** Agents who are instructed on a multiple agency basis are often reluctant to spend money advertising and marketing a property which might be sold by a competitor. Your property will probably get far more exposure if you instruct an agent on a sole agency basis.

- **No risk of overexposure**. If a potential purchaser is offered the same property by ten different agents, he may wonder what is wrong with it. There is no doubt that overexposure can be counter-productive. A sole agency will avoid this problem.

- **No conflict of interest**. Imagine a situation where an agent receives a low offer for your property. If he is acting as your sole agent he can safely advise you to refuse it. If he is acting on a multiple agency basis he might be tempted to try to persuade you to accept the low offer to ensure that he gets the fee, not his competitor.

For these reasons I would advise most sellers to start off by instructing an agent on a sole agency basis. The exceptions are detailed below.

Circumstances where a joint sole agency is appropriate
People who are looking for a very expensive or unusual house are usually prepared to consider properties in a much larger geographical area than most ordinary purchasers.

A purchaser who wants to buy a country estate, a listed property or perhaps a riverside property, might be prepared to look at anything within, say, two hours' travelling time of London. Such purchasers could not possibly register with all the agents in such a large area and most will therefore register their requirements only with agents in London and the major provincial cities. Unless your property is being offered for sale at these locations it will be overlooked.

If your property is truly unusual, it is well worth the extra expense of a joint sole agency. If it is not, the extra commission payable (typically 30 – 50 per cent more) is unlikely to be recovered.

Circumstances where a multiple agency is appropriate
Despite the inherent disadvantages of multiple agency there are some circumstances in which it might be appropriate:

- **For village or suburban properties**. Some village and suburban properties require exposure in more than one local town or centre. If you are selling a property in a village that is equidistant from three or more larger towns, you might consider instructing one agent in each centre on a multiple agency basis. Where there are only two local towns a joint sole agency agreement may be more appropriate.

- **When no agent in the town is outstanding**. Perhaps you can't make up your mind between instructing a small enthusiastic independent agent or a larger but apparently less efficient one. If you really can't decide, a multiple agency might be appropriate.

● **When a property has already been unsuccessfully marketed by a sole agent**. This is the most common reason for instructing an agent on a multiple agency basis. Although multiple agency is often appropriate in these circumstances, you should also consider sacking the first agent and entering into a second sole agency agreement with another firm.

The one thing to avoid at all costs is the temptation to instruct every agent in the town. In a town with 20 agents there is nothing to be gained from instructing more than two or three. If you instruct all 20, your property will be overexposed and your chances of selling it seriously reduced.

Northern England

Circumstances where an exclusive sole agency is appropriate
As an *exclusive* agency client you will be responsible for paying all out-of-pocket expenses involved with marketing your property whether it is sold or not. As an *inclusive* agency client you will, through higher fee levels, end up paying not only the costs of marketing your property, but also a proportion of the cost of marketing other properties that were withdrawn from the market leaving the agent with unrecoverable costs to bear. For this reason exclusive agency is usually the most cost-effective choice for the committed vendor.

Circumstances where an inclusive sole agency is appropriate
There are two circumstances where an inclusive agency might be appropriate:

(1) When you are not certain about an agent's ability.

(2) Where there is a chance that you might change your mind about moving. (In which case is it really fair to waste the agent's time and money?)

INSTRUCTING AN ESTATE AGENT

Giving detailed instructions
Having made your decision regarding which agent to instruct and on

what terms, you should next clarify in your mind your detailed instructions to that agent. In particular you need to make a decision on:

Initial asking price
Bearing in mind all the evidence that you have seen and heard, are you certain about your initial asking price? If it is too high, it will spoil the momentum of the marketing campaign and may demotivate the agent. On the other hand, if it is too low, it will be all but impossible to raise it later.

Period of sole agency
What period of sole agency are you prepared to give? If it is too short (say less than six weeks) the agent may be reluctant to spend money marketing a property that he might not sell. If it is too long (say more than twelve weeks) you run the risk of being tied to an ineffective agent.

Subagencies
Some agents will invite other agents in the town to act on a subagency basis. This means that they will also offer your property for sale and if they sell it will receive half the commission. My opinion is that subagencies are usually not in the best interests of the seller, mainly because of the risk of overexposure. If you are prepared to allow your agent to instruct subagents, you should insist that the number is strictly limited and ask for a list of all subagents before they are instructed.

For Sale board
Approximately 25 per cent of all potential buyers are attracted by For Sale boards and a board will therefore undoubtedly increase your chances of selling. If you are reluctant to have one, you should examine your objections most carefully. Is the risk of the odd unwanted caller a price worth paying for a quicker sale?

Keys
If at all possible you should give your agent a key. This is even more important if you are out at work in the daytime. A surprising number of people prefer to view during working hours and many will not bother to try to make another appointment if they cannot view immediately.

Having made a decision on all the above issues you are now ready to telephone the lucky agent to inform him of your decision and arrange a final appointment to put the house on the market.

Informing the unsuccessful agents

It is well worth spending five or ten minutes telephoning or writing to the unsuccessful agents to inform them of your decision. You might need their services in the future and a short courtesy call at this time will make it far easier to go back to them should the need arise.

UNDERSTANDING THE SOLE AGENCY AGREEMENT

The agency agreement is a legal contract and you should read it most carefully before signing. You should not hesitate to ask the agent to explain any clause that is unclear. If you are not happy with any aspect of the agreement you should refuse to sign it on the spot and take it to your solicitor or to a trusted friend for clarification.

A typical agency agreement will include the following:

- **Confirmation of fee level.** Check that this is what has been agreed. Also check any multiple agency rate. It will be far easier to negotiate a multiple agency rate now, when the sole agency period is being agreed, than later when it is being ended.

- **Confirmation of asking price.** Double check the figure agreed.

- **Confirmation of agency terms.** Check that you are signing for a sole or multiple agency as appropriate.

- **Sole agency period.** Check that this is as agreed. Check also whether a notice period is hidden in the small print.

- **Authority to pay fees.** Many agency agreements contain a clause that gives your solicitor authority to pay the agent's fees from the sale proceeds.

- **Offer of 'connected services'.** Estate agents must by law inform you of any service that might be offered to potential purchasers such as mortgage advice, removals or the sale of their own property.

- **For Sale board.** Many agency agreements include a clause authorising the erection of a For Sale board. Delete this clause if you don't want one.

- **Race Relations Act.** Many agreements include a clause that confirms that you will not discriminate against potential purchasers on account of their colour or race.

- **Subagencies.** Many agreements include a clause that gives the agent authority to instruct subagents. Delete this if appropriate.

- **Property Misdescriptions Act.** You may be asked to sign a separate form relating to the Property Misdescriptions Act.

- **Other specific instructions.** You should insist that any additional instructions given to the agent are recorded in writing on the sole agency agreement to prevent misunderstandings.

A sample sole agency agreement is shown in Appendix 1.

CASE STUDY

James and Tina instruct three agents

James and Tina were in a great hurry to sell their flat in London so they decided to instruct three agents on a multi-agency basis. This tactic seemed to pay off and ten viewings were arranged for the first weekend. The problems started on Monday when all three agents said that they had a buyer who was prepared to offer the full asking price.

James and Tina asked for details about the position of each buyer and on the basis of what they were told they decided to accept an offer from a nice young couple who had sold their own property and said that they would be ready to exchange contracts within three weeks.

Five weeks later little progress had been made so James and Tina asked their solicitor to investigate the reason for the delay. He made enquiries and reported back that the nice young couple had lost the buyer for their own property and were trying to find another. Their sale had in fact fallen through nearly five weeks previously.

James and Tina were furious. They rang their agent and accused him of not supervising the sale closely enough. Their agent replied that it was not his fault if someone told him lies. James and Tina withdrew from the sale and sold instead through another agent to one of the other people who had made an offer five weeks previously. They were left with a bill for abortive costs of nearly £400.

James and Tina suspect that their first agent deliberately withheld information about their buyers' sale falling through because he did not want to risk losing his commission, but they know that they will never be able to prove this.

Commenting on his experience James said, 'next time we will instruct just one agent, then we will know that they are acting in our interest not theirs'.

CHECKLIST

All estate agents are not the same.

The comparison table in Figure 1 will help you to assess the agents that you have seen. Give each agent a score out of ten in each category.

INITIAL IMPRESSIONS		Agent				
MARKETING CAMPAIGN		1	2	3	4	5
Newspaper advertising						
1	Size of advert					
2	Quality of publication					
3	Position					
4	Frequency					
5	Layout					
6	Colour/black & white					
7	Variety/content					
8	Sale board presence					
9	Office position					
10	Overall impression					
CUSTOMER SERVICE						
11	Initial response					
12	Rapport					
13	Qualification					
14	Sales ability					
15	Quality of property details					
16	Promptness					
17	Presentation					
18	Telephone follow-up					
19	Ongoing follow-up					
20	Persistence					
21	Overall impression					

Fig. 1. Comparison table for short listed agents.

MARKETING CAMPAIGN	1	2	3	4	5
THE VALUATION APPOINTMENT					
1 First impressions					
2 Thoroughness of background research					
3 Accuracy of valuation					
4 Presentation of valuation					
5 Sales presentation					
6 Experience					
7 Company background					
8 Advertising					
9 Quality of particulars					
10 Coverage					
11 Opening hours					
12 Sales methods					
13 Buyer qualification					
14 Sales progressing					
15 Recent results					
16 Testimonials					
Fee Levels %					
Non-conventional fee alternatives					
Minimum period of sole agency requested (weeks)					
Overall score					

Fig. 1. Continued.

4
Finding a Buyer

PREPARING THE PARTICULARS

The first thing that your estate agent will do after instructions have been confirmed is to prepare the **property particulars**.

The particulars will play an extremely important role in persuading potential purchasers to view your property. It is, therefore, worth going to some considerable trouble to ensure that they show the property to its best advantage.

The following tips will help to ensure that your particulars stand out from the crowd.

General layout

The typical purchaser will receive several dozen sets of particulars during his property search. Because of this, your particulars will need to make their impact within just a few seconds. Sloppy photocopying or poor layout will reduce significantly the number of potential buyers who decide to view and should not be tolerated.

The photograph

Ninety per cent of purchasers will look at the photograph before they look at anything else. If they don't like what they see, they will reject your property out of hand. It is therefore vital to ensure that the photograph shows your property in the best possible light.

Choosing an angle

The angle that the photograph is taken from should be chosen with particular care. Most photographs show the front elevation. However, if your property looks better from another angle, there is no reason why the photograph should not show the back or the side.

Colour v black and white

The photograph itself really should be in colour. If your estate agent does not use colour photographs on his details, it is worth considering paying the extra cost of colour photography yourself.

Size
The size of the photograph is important. A photograph that measures 5" x 7" or larger will make a far greater impact than the traditional mini print.

Recency
The last point to make about the photograph is that it must be recent. A photograph sent out in August of a property covered in snow will convey the message 'and they *still* haven't sold it!'

Internal photographs
Internal photographs can play a useful role in persuading people to view a property. If your property has any particularly attractive internal features, you should ask your estate agent to include an internal photograph on the details.

Photographing ugly properties
Some houses are not particularly photogenic. Some houses are just plain ugly. If your property falls into this category (be honest with yourself here) it may be better to include only internal photographs on the property particulars.

The text
You must always remember that the purpose of the particulars is to persuade people to view your property, not to sell the property itself. You should therefore be ruthless about removing from the text all unnecessary information. In particular you should take care to remove any trivial details that might discourage people from viewing. For example, reference to a pink bathroom suite would do nothing to increase a property's saleability but could, very easily, put some purchasers off.

Property particulars and the law
Estate agents used to be famous for their ability to make even the most undesirable property sound like a palace. All such hyperbole was ended by the passing of the Property Misdescriptions Act in April 1993.

The Property Misdescriptions Act made it a *criminal* offence for an estate agent (but not a homeowner) to misdescribe a property that is offered for sale. The penalties for non-compliance are severe and even a minor transgression can lead to a substantial fine and a criminal record for the estate agent.

How the Act affects you

The passing of the Property Misdescriptions Act has led to far-reaching changes in estate agency practice and this has affected vendors in two ways. The first effect of the Act is that estate agents' details have become far shorter and less colourful than they used to be. Estate agents dare not make any statement that cannot be verified. Thus a phrase such as 'the house is ten minutes' walk from the shops' has either been changed to 'the property is 637 metres from the nearest shop' or, more commonly, omitted altogether.

The second effect of the Act has been to cause considerable delays in putting properties onto the market. The reason for this is that estate agents now have a statutory obligation to verify all claims that they wish to make about a property. For example, if a property has been rewired the agent will need to see a detailed invoice for the work. If a property has damp guarantees the agent will need to see a copy. If a property has a 67-year lease, the agent will need to see a copy of the lease to verify this. Many homeowners do not have such documents readily available and the delays that occur while the documents are obtained can cause considerable inconvenience and frustration. If you find yourself in this situation, you will need to choose between waiting for the documents to be obtained, and marketing your property with all reference to the unsubstantiated facts omitted from the details.

GETTING PEOPLE TO VIEW

What should the agent be doing?

Once the house is on the market your agent should start earning his fee by persuading as many people as possible to view it. He will try to achieve this in a number of ways.

By telephone

The agent should have a number of 'hot applicants' on his register. These are people who are prepared to view without seeing the details and are in a position to proceed with a purchase immediately (first time buyers or own property sold). The agent should telephone these people to obtain viewings *before* the details are sent out. These are the hottest applicants of all. One of them may want to buy your property immediately.

By post
During the preceding two to three months the agent's general marketing campaign should have attracted a number of applicants. Within the first few days, the agent should send a set of particulars to every applicant that he has in the price range. Sending details alone is not enough. The effective agent will also telephone each of these applicants a few days after they receive the details to obtain feedback and to attempt to persuade them to view.

Circulating details to other branches
If you have instructed a multi-office agent, details of your property should be circulated to all the neighbouring branches. This will not always happen automatically. Inter-branch rivalry often means that neighbouring branches end up competing with each other rather than cooperating. You can check whether such inter-branch rivalries might affect your chances of obtaining a sale by doing two things: first, ask what commission sharing arrangements are in place in the event of your property being sold by another branch (do they seem fair to you?). Secondly, try phoning the neighbouring branches posing as an applicant looking for a property in the same price range as yours and see whether your property is mentioned.

Erecting a For Sale board
A For Sale board is an important marketing tool. Something like a quarter of all sales are achieved due to a board. If you really want to sell your house for the best possible price in the shortest possible time, then you need a For Sale board. The board may encourage the odd unwanted visitor to knock on the door without an appointment, but such people can easily be politely turned away and this small intrusion is a price well worth paying for the extra interest that a board will generate.

How long should it take to find a buyer?
It is, of course, impossible to predict how long it will take to find a buyer. The report produced by Black Horse Agencies (see Appendix 2) gives some idea of the average time it takes to sell a property. However, there is a big difference between the average time it takes to sell a property and how long it takes the average property to sell. The reason for this is that a property that takes two years to sell will have a disproportionate effect on the average.

Statistically the time when a property in Southern England is most likely to sell is during the first four weeks of going onto the market. During this period the agent is able to work on all the potential buyers

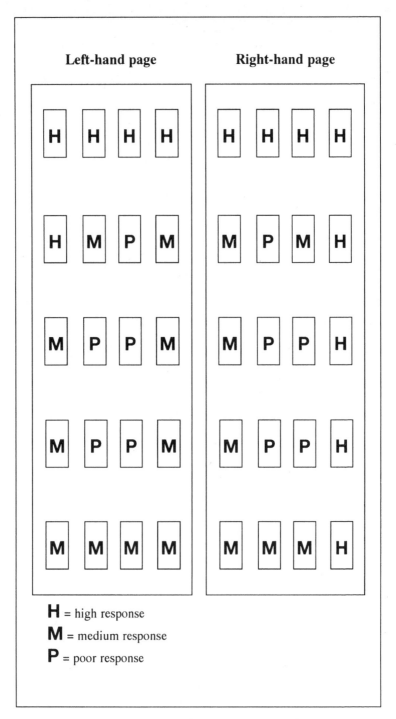

Fig. 2. Choosing the best position for your advertisement.

who have registered during the preceding few months. By the end of the first month you should certainly have had a number of viewings and you may well have achieved a sale.

In Northern England, as the report shows, the market tends to operate more slowly. If you are selling a property in the north you should allow eight to twelve weeks for the initial marketing campaign to run its course.

If you have not achieved a sale within these time-scales, you should begin to consider the possibility that your property is going to prove more difficult to sell than you first thought.

RUNNING THE ADVERTISING CAMPAIGN

The advertising campaign is a very important part of the overall marketing plan. The following hints will help to ensure that you get maximum benefit from the advertisements that are run for your property.

Page position

Certain positions on the page attract far more interest than others. In general terms the rules are:

● Right-hand pages are better than left-hand pages.

● The top of the page is better than the bottom of the page.

● The boxes at the edge of a page attract more interest than those in the centre of the page.

This can be shown as a diagram (see Figure 2).

Try to insist on a good position when your property is advertised. A good position could double or treble the response.

The photograph

Potential buyers will look at the photograph and decide whether or not they want to view the property within seconds. It is therefore essential to choose a photograph that shows the property in its best light. If you have any reservations about the photograph you should not hesitate to ask your agent to take another one.

First advertisement Appeals to family with children	**Close to Queens School** This three bedroom semi-detached property is situated in a quiet cul-de-sac and is very convenient to Queens School. It has three bedrooms and a 60' south facing garden. Price £69,950.
Second advertisement Appeals to professional couple	**First class commuter access** This three bedroom semi-detached property is within two minutes of the M1, Junction 10 and less than half a mile from the mainline station. The accommodation comprises three bedrooms and two separate reception rooms. The property is in excellent condition throughout. Price £69,950.
Third advertisement Appeals to gardeners	**South facing garden** This three bedroom, two reception property is in first class condition throughout. A particular feature is the well stocked 60' south facing garden which has been lovingly tended by the present owners. Price £69,950.

Fig. 3. Changing the text of your advertisement.

Subsequent photographs
Many buyers have a memory like an elephant for houses that have been previously advertised. If they recognise a photograph that they have seen before, they will move straight on to the next property without even pausing to read the text.

The golden rule therefore is never to use the same photograph twice. Subsequent advertisements should use a photograph taken from a different angle, an internal shot or perhaps a rear view of the property.

Advertising an ugly property

There is little point in photographing an ugly property. If your house looks like a concrete prison block you should consider:

● advertising it with an internal photograph

● advertising it without a photograph at all

● asking your agent to advertise a prettier property in the same price range as your own on the understanding that all respondents will be told about your property as well as the one advertised.

The text

The purpose of an advertisement is to generate enquiries. If everything that a potential purchaser needs to know about the property is included in the advertisement then they will have no reason to contact the agent. The effective agent will counter this by withholding a vital piece of information about each property. This might be the location, the price or the number of bedrooms.

By advertising in this way, the agent can increase quite significantly the number of enquiries that each advertisement generates. Once a prospective purchaser is on the phone the agent will have a much better chance of persuading him to view the property.

Text of subsequent advertisements
An advertisement that has been run once is stale. If the same advertisement is run again it will achieve a much reduced response. You should, therefore, never use the same text twice. Subsequent advertisements should be rewritten from scratch and should highlight different features of the property. For example, see Figure 3.

Setting an advertising budget

In Southern England, the cost of local property advertising is usually included in the agency fee. In Northern England many agents charge for all advertising and will want to agree an advertising budget with you at the time of instruction.

You should be aware that many agents make a profit from selling you advertising space and therefore have an incentive to sell you as much as possible. You should be cautious about agreeing to a major advertising campaign straight away. For most properties a budget that covers three or four local advertisements should be sufficient. If necessary, the budget can always be reviewed at a later date.

National advertising

For most properties a local advertising campaign will be sufficient. However, some properties will benefit from further exposure in a regional, national or specialist publication. Such properties might include:

- high value properties

- waterside properties

- properties with equestrian facilities

- properties that might have an appeal as a holiday home

- highly unusual/individual properties

- properties with potential for dual residential/commercial usage

- properties with investment/lettings potential.

If your property falls into one of these categories, you should ask your agent to advise you on the cost of an advertising campaign in the appropriate publications. The cost of such advertising is nearly always borne by the vendor, not the agent.

Editorial coverage

Most local property newspapers have an editorial section which features a small number of properties each week. Most papers give each of the agents space in the editorial section on a rota basis. Editorials often generate far more enquiries for a property than an ordinary advertisement and it would be well worth trying to persuade your agent to include your property in their next editorial feature.

Open house

A more unconventional approach to advertising is the open house. For some reason many purchasers are far more willing to attend an open house than to arrange a specific appointment to view a property. Perhaps they feel under less pressure. Perhaps they don't want to commit themselves to a precise time. Whatever the reason, advertising an open house can generate far more interest than a conventional advertisement.

The house is advertised as usual except that the times of the open house are prominently displayed. Some open house advertisements include the full address. In other cases the address is withheld so that the agent can take the applicant's details and verify them to be genuine prior to the viewing.

Coming soon advertisements

A variation on the open house idea is the 'coming soon' advertisement. This is effectively a teaser campaign. Advertisements appear over a period of two to three weeks that say:

Coming Soon

Four bedroom detached property in Lincoln's Fields area. The property is in need of some updating and refurbishment. Price guide £100,000.

Buyers who respond to the advertisement are all invited to view the property on a predetermined date at a predetermined time. No one is allowed to see the property until this time. The effect of several buyers arriving at once is that the property appears to be in great demand. As a result it is often possible to achieve a premium price.

SHOWING PEOPLE AROUND

Who should conduct the viewings?

An estate agent will nearly always show a house more effectively than the owner could themselves. There are two reasons for this:

1. Purchasers are more likely to tell the agent what they *really* think of a property. This feedback helps the agent to overcome objections.

2. Experience will have taught the agent how to show each property to its best advantage.

You should therefore ask your agent to accompany as many viewings as possible, even if they are at a time when you will be at home yourselves.

Preparing for a viewing

A well conducted viewing should aim to appeal to at least three of the five senses:

Sight

- Try to ensure that the house is as tidy as possible.

- Draw all the curtains right back from the windows to make the rooms appear bigger and brighter.

- On dull days turn all the lights on – electric light is much warmer and more friendly than daylight (although sunlight is best of all).

- In spring, autumn or winter light a fire if you have one.

Sound

- Turn the television off. It makes people feel that they are intruding.

- Put some background music on quietly (classical is best).

- Close the windows if the house is affected by any sort of background noise (traffic, trains, *etc*).

Smell

- Attractive smells can make a very positive impression – coffee brewing, bread baking, food cooking are all homely and atmospheric.

- Unpleasant smells can be very off-putting; these include dogs, tobacco, air fresheners and dirty bins.

Atmosphere

I was once told a story about a beautiful flat that had failed to sell after more than a hundred viewings. Eventually the agent discovered that the reason was that the vendors (who were divorcing) were showing purchasers round in an atmosphere that was so poisonous that all the viewers wanted to do was get out. By conducting viewings whilst the vendors were out the agent was able to obtain an offer within a few days.

Dogs

A barking dog is for many people a most unpleasant first impression of the property. Try to take the dog out for a walk when a viewing is expected. If that is not possible, shut the dog in the car or in a back room until the potential purchasers have left.

When the agent is conducting the viewing
Your role
If the agent is conducting the viewing the best thing that you can do is to go out. If that is not possible, the next best thing is to stay out of the way (preferably in one of the less attractive rooms) until the agent has left. The agent will introduce you to the purchasers when they view the room that you are in but otherwise it is best for you to play no part in the proceedings.

Conducting a viewing yourself
The following hints will help you to make the best of every viewing:

Preparation
Ask the agent about the purchaser's background – their job, hobbies, *etc.* It is much easier to strike up a conversation with someone when you know something about them. Ask the agent also about the purchaser's main requirements (*eg* large garden, lots of space downstairs, low maintenance, *etc*). This will enable you to stress these key points during the viewing.

Greeting
First impressions really do count. Smile when you greet the purchasers – it can make a real difference.

One of you or two
Only one of you should conduct the viewing. Your partner will only get in the way and make the rooms seem smaller.

Order of rooms
Show the buyer the best room first. Take them round the rest of the house in a logical order then end up in the best room again at the end. This will mean that their first and last impression is a good one.

After you
A room always seems bigger when it is empty. You should therefore always let purchasers enter each room first.

Don't talk too much
Many vendors, perhaps through nervousness, point out every power point and dimmer switch. This can be most off-putting. It's really best to say as little as possible. You should, however:

● Relate the house to the purchaser's requirements, *eg* I understand you wanted a big garden. This is one and a quarter acres.

● Point out things the purchasers might not notice themselves, *eg* you could knock the pantry through to make a breakfast area here.

 Create a warm atmosphere by saying things like how happy you have been in the house.

Privacy
Couples need time alone to discuss the house before they leave. The best way to achieve this is to send them out to look at the garden on their own.

Security
These days you cannot be too careful. I was once told a story about a purchaser with several million pounds to spend, who was seen to steal a bottle of perfume during an accompanied viewing. Keep your eyes open and never leave purchasers alone in the house.

Handling questions
Be cautious about answering questions like 'Why are you moving?' It is so easy to put purchasers off.

Dealing with rude people
You may meet someone who spends the whole visit being rude about your house. It really is best to ignore such comments unless the provocation is extreme. Some people are just rude by nature. Others may actually be interested in the property and might be trying to talk the price down.

Handling offers
On no account should you get embroiled in price negotiations yourself.

It is so easy to say something that you later regret. If a purchaser makes an offer, whatever it is, thank them enthusiastically and refer them to the agent.

At the end of the viewing
However uninterested the purchasers appear, end the viewing by offering them a chance to go round again and/or to come back for a second look.

Obtaining feedback
The agent should let you know what every purchaser thought within 48 hours of the viewing. If they do not, ring them.

Prepare for disappointments
Purchasers are often quite nervous when they are viewing someone's house and some cover up this nervousness by saying how lovely everything is. This doesn't mean they want to buy it. Be prepared to find that many promising viewings do not result in an offer.

Maintain your enthusiasm
No matter how many people you have shown round, it is vital to maintain your enthusiasm. I have known of many cases where houses have failed to sell because their owners (or agents) have grown sick of showing people around. If you do not seem interested in selling the property no purchaser will wish to buy it.

CASE STUDY

Getting the right photograph

Lydia was horrified to see the way in which her agent had prepared particulars of her property. The photograph was in black and white, not colour as she had been promised, and it was taken from a most unattractive angle that made her property appear far smaller than it really was. No wonder she had had so few viewings.

Lydia complained to her estate agent, who took a new photograph, added some internal shots and produced the full colour details that she had been promised. The number of viewings increased immediately and an offer was agreed two weeks later.

CHECKLIST

● Have you seen the particulars? Are you happy with them, particularly the photographs?

- Have you checked to make sure that your agent intends to follow-up every set of particulars sent out with a phone call?

- Has your agent ordered a For Sale board?

- Have you agreed an advertising schedule?

- Does your property warrant regional or national advertising?

- Have you received feedback on what each viewer thought of your property?

5
Reviewing Progress

ARRANGING THE FIRST REVIEW MEETING

Your house has been on the market for about four weeks (eight weeks in the north). It has been advertised, details have been sent out, and purchasers have been telephoned. You may well have had some viewings but there is still no sign of a buyer.

If this is the stage that you have reached, then it is time to visit your agent for a review meeting. Telephone your agent, tell him that you are concerned that the property has not yet sold and ask for an appointment to discuss what else can be done. Try not to get drawn into a discussion over the telephone. A review meeting really is something that needs to be handled face to face.

Has the property been properly marketed?

Start the review meeting by asking your agent, in a non-confrontational way, why he thinks that your property has not yet sold. Whatever answer he gives, you should ask him next to go through everything that he has already done to find a buyer. In particular you should ask about:

●   **Feedback from existing viewings**. What comments have been made by the people who have viewed? Is there one thing that is putting people off? Could anything be done to change it?

●   **Mail outs**. Ask how many sets of details have been sent out.

●   **Phone outs**. Ask how many people have been telephoned to try to obtain a viewing. Ask what comments were made about the property by people who did not wish to view it. Again, is one thing putting people off? Could something be done to change it?

●   **Other branches**. Check to ensure that any other local branches have details of your property.

- **Advertising**. Ask to see copies of all advertisements for your property. Are you satisfied these show your property to the best advantage?

- **Details**. Ask to see a copy of the details again. Are they still as well presented as the first set you saw?

Reviewing the asking price

The value of any property is ultimately determined by the price of the properties that are currently competing for the same buyers. The properties that are available change all the time and this means that the value of your property can fluctuate. If, for example, the house next door to you is put on the market for £5,000 less than yours, it will make it much more difficult to achieve your asking price. In order to check that your asking price is still realistic you should:

- Ask to see full details of all houses that the agent has sold in the same price range, whilst your property has been on the market. How do they compare with your own?

- Ask to see details of all other houses that the agent is currently marketing in the same price range. These properties will be competing directly with yours for the same buyers. How do they compare?

- Go through the current issue of the property newspaper with your agent. Are any of the properties advertised by other agents better value than your own?

In the light of such evidence you may need to consider reducing the asking price.

What else can be done to find a buyer?

If you are certain that the asking price is correct, you might ask your agent to take all or some of the following actions:

- **Prepare new particulars**. By taking new photographs and rewriting the particulars an old property can be made to seem like a new instruction. Sometimes this will result in viewings from people who were put off by something in the original particulars.

- Ask the agent to send **every member of his sales team** to see your property. They may be more enthusiastic about selling a property that they have seen themselves.

- **Readvertise**. Try to find a different aspect to feature – perhaps the garden, the history of the house, anything to make it appeal to a different group of purchasers.

- Consider **national or regional advertising**. For many properties national advertising produces disappointing results. However, it might be worth considering one advert to test the market in a larger geographical area.

- **Increased incentive**. Consider offering a bonus of say half a per cent to the individual negotiator who sells the property. This can transform their motivation! You will need the approval of the branch manager or proprietor.

Changing agents

You may discover during the review meeting that your agent has not been doing his job effectively. If this is the case, you must tell him why you are dissatisfied. This is not a time to beat about the bush.

Four weeks is probably too soon to consider changing agents but, if you have good cause for dissatisfaction, it might be the best thing to do. However, before you disinstruct your agent, you should check carefully the terms of any sole agency agreement that you have signed. If you do not you could find yourself liable to pay two lots of agency fees.

DECIDING WHAT TO DO IF IT STILL WON'T SELL

Around eight weeks (16 in the north) have passed and there is still no sign of a buyer. What should be done next?

Arrange a second review meeting

The first thing to do is to arrange a second review meeting with the estate agent. This should be conducted in a very similar way to the first one:

- Ask the agent why he thinks your property hasn't sold.

- Ask what comments have been made by people who have viewed – is one thing putting them off?

- Ask how many sets of details have been sent out.

- Ask how many people have been told about the house on the telephone.

- Ask what comments have been made by buyers who did not want to view, having seen the details. Is one thing putting them off?

- Check that the property has been circulated to any other local branches.

- Ask to see copies of advertising for the property run since the last review meeting.

- Ask to see a copy of the details again.

- Ask the agent again if he will accompany all viewings if he is not already doing so.

- Consider rewriting the details if you have not already done so.

- Consider a For Sale board if you don't already have one.

- Consider an open house, if you haven't already tried one.

- Ask the agent to send every member of the sales team to view the house for themselves.

REVIEWING THE ASKING PRICE

If the property has not sold after eight weeks it could well be that the asking price is too high. Try to assess this by:

- Asking to see details of all other properties in the same price range as yours.

- Asking to see details of properties that the agent has sold in the same price range since the last review meeting.

- Looking at the price of any similar properties to your own that have been advertised in the newspaper.

Try to be honest with yourself and ask how your property compares with the competition.

CHECKING UP ON YOUR AGENT

If you are certain that the asking price is realistic, the next thing to do is check up on how well your agent is marketing your property. This can be done in a number of ways:

- Ask a friend to register with your agent as a buyer for a property like yours. What sort of service do they get? Is your property promoted both on the telephone and by the sending out of written particulars?

- Ask your friend to arrange to actually view your property with your estate agent. How well do they feel that the property is being sold?

- Phone the agent yourself to enquire about a property that has been advertised at a similar price to your own. Is your property also mentioned?

- Phone the agent and say that you have seen a For Sale board outside your house. Does the agent really push hard to try to get a viewing?

If such tests reveal that your property is still being effectively marketed then there is no alternative but to be patient. If not the time may have come to change agents.

CASE STUDY

Learning the value of a review meeting

Sanjay and Monisha had been trying to sell their five-bedroom property in the Midlands for three months without success. They could not understand why their property had failed to sell so they arranged a review meeting with their agent. They were horrified by what they found.

The particulars which had originally featured full colour photographs now had a poor quality black and white photocopy of the original photographs. When they asked their agent what the viewers had said about their house it was clear that he had never bothered to follow the viewings up so he did not know. Furthermore the national advertisement that they had been promised had not been run.

Sanjay and Monisha made their dissatisfaction clear and told their agent that if he did not address their concerns immediately they would withdraw their property.

Their agent took a new photograph, prepared new particulars, sent them out to everyone on the mailing list again and followed up with a phone call. Within two weeks nine viewings had been arranged and an offer had been agreed at close to the asking price.

CHECKLIST

● Do you know how many sets of particulars have been sent out?

● Has your agent followed up every set of particulars with a phone call?

● Do you know what every viewer has said about your property?

● Is the asking price correct? Have you checked this out by looking at the price of similar properties that are currently for sale?

● Have you checked up on your agent by registering as a buyer for a property like yours? Is he really doing what he says he is doing?

6
Changing Your Estate Agent

The time may come when you have to accept that your first agent is not going to find a buyer within a reasonable period of time.

Once you reach this point, your first decision is whether to instruct a second agent as well as or instead of the first one.

CONSIDERING SOLE AGENCY v MULTIPLE AGENCY

The main arguments are:

- multiple agency encourages agents to work for themselves, not for you

- overexposure of the property can reduce the chances of finding a buyer

- multiple agency is more expensive

- a sole agent has more incentive to work harder to achieve a sale.

For all these reasons the best course of action in most situations is to disinstruct the first agent and to appoint the new agent on a sole agency basis.

DISINSTRUCTING AN AGENT

Disinstructing an agent is probably best done over the telephone. Thank the agent for his work in trying to find a buyer and tell him that you are sorry that he was not successful. Then tell him politely, but firmly, that you will now be instructing another agent and that you would like him to take the property off his books. You should expect the agent to try to persuade you to stick with him for a little longer and he may even offer incentives, such as extra advertising, to persuade you to do so. You should not be swayed.

71

Contractual obligations

Your sole agency agreement may impose contractual obligations on you and you should check it carefully before disinstructing your agent. Common obligations would be:

● **A notice period for disinstruction** (typically two weeks) may be required.

● **Withdrawal fee.** Many agents, particularly in the north of England, will charge a withdrawal fee if they are disinstructed for any reason. This could be several hundred pounds.

● **Out-of-pocket expenses.** Many agents, again particularly in the north of England, require reimbursement of all outstanding expenses such as advertising, colour photography, *etc*, at the time of disinstruction.

Breaking a sole agency agreement

If you granted the agent a period of sole agency you will usually be contractually obliged to honour it. If the property is sold by another agent within the sole agency period you could find yourself liable to pay two agency fees. You might try to persuade the original agent to release you from the agency agreement by pointing out that he has nothing to gain from keeping a dissatisfied vendor on his books. However, the agent is not obliged to release you from the agreement early and, if he will not, you have no choice but to delay instructing the new agent until after the original agreement has expired.

Avoiding commission disputes

A fee will be payable to the first agent in the event that the property is sold to a buyer who has previously viewed it through that agent. To avoid arguments in the future it is as well to write to your agent to ask him to do two things:

1.   Confirm that he has taken the property off the market.

2.   Provide a list of the names of all purchasers who have viewed through him.

INSTRUCTING A SECOND AGENT

Choosing an agent

The most obvious agent to instruct the second time round will be the runner-up in your original beauty contest. However, this decision should not be an automatic one. If another agent has sold a lot of houses in your area during the time that yours has been on the market, then it would be well worth asking that agent to value your property before you make a final decision.

Booking the appointment
All the local agents will know that your property has been on the market and there is nothing to gain from trying to hide this. However, it is important that the agent should not think that the appointment is a guaranteed instruction. If he does he may send a junior member of staff to take the details. To avoid this you should tell him on the phone that:

- you wish to instruct a new agent on a sole not a multiple agency basis

- you need advice on the asking price and would like to see details of similar properties in the same price range (both sold and available).

Preparing for the appointment
You should prepare for the agent's visit in the same way as you would for any other viewing. Agents are human too, and their valuation will be affected by how well the property is presented.

Establishing the ground rules
The agent will often expect an appointment at a house that is already on the market to be a guaranteed instruction. You should make it clear at the beginning of the appointment that this is not the case. Tell the agent that you are disappointed that the first company that you instructed did not find a buyer and that you are anxious not to make another mistake.

The agent's sales presentation
Having agreed on an asking price, the next stage is to ask the agent what he will do differently from the first agent to market the property. In particular ask him:

- how he will present the particulars differently

- how and where he will advertise

- how many purchasers he has on his books

- why he thinks the house has not sold already

- what other properties have recently sold in the same price range.

Negotiating a fee

You will be in a weaker position to negotiate a fee than you were the last time around. The agent will know that your property has proved to be difficult to sell and will therefore quite probably hold out for a higher fee. However, this does not mean that you have to accept whatever fee is offered. You might suggest that you have an alternative agent in mind whom you will instruct if an agreement cannot be reached.

The sole agency contract

Don't be pressurised into signing an agreement on the spot. If you have any doubts ask the agent to leave the agreement with you.

The sole agency period

The period of sole agency should be similar to the period given to the original agent – eight weeks would be typical. Any less and the agent will be reluctant to spend money marketing a property that he may not sell. Any more and you run the risk of being stuck with an ineffective agent.

Instructing an agent on a multiple agency basis

There are circumstances where it is appropriate to instruct a second agent on a multiple basis. Perhaps the second agent is based in another town or suburb or advertises in a different newspaper. However, a third agent will very seldom do anything to increase your chances and fourth or fifth may actually make it more difficult to find a buyer. However desperate you are to sell I would urge you not to overexpose the property.

What to do if it still won't sell

Hard as it is to accept, you have now done everything that can be done. If you are not willing or able to be patient, the only thing left to do is begin reducing the asking price until you reach the figure at which the property sells immediately. Be warned, this could be many thousands of pounds less than its true value.

CASE STUDY

Changing agents pays dividends

Stuart and Linda were very disappointed with their original estate agent. When they went to see him to find out why their property had not sold it quickly became clear than he had not been doing his job properly. Stuart and Linda felt badly let down and gave their agent notice that they would be terminating their sole agency agreement when it expired.

Their second agent was by comparison a model of efficiency. The details were better, they had a much more proactive approach to persuading people to view on the telephone and they phoned the next day to report on the feedback from each viewing. Within a week an offer had been agreed. Stuart and Linda were amused to find that their buyer had also been registered with the original agent who had failed to either send them details or contact them by telephone – poetic justice indeed.

CHECKLIST

● How long was the original sole agency agreement that you signed? Can you give notice to terminate it early?

● What notice period must you give to end the agency agreement?

● What fees and expenses are you likely to pay if you withdraw the property?

● Have you confirmed the termination of your agreement in writing and listed the names of all viewers in order to avoid future commission disputes?

● Have you taken the necessary steps to ensure that the second agent will be better than the first?

7
Dealing with Offers

PREPARING TO NEGOTIATE

At last the moment you have been waiting for has arrived – you have received an offer. Unfortunately you cannot afford to breathe a sigh of relief just yet. A great deal of care will still be necessary in order to ensure that the best possible selling price is achieved and that the sale goes through to a successful completion. Three general principles will help to ensure that your negotiations have the very best chance of reaching a satisfactory conclusion:

1.   Don't handle negotiations yourself.

2.   Don't take offence at low offers.

3.   Do conduct negotiations in writing.

Don't handle negotiations yourself

Whatever the temptation, you should never handle negotiations yourself. Your estate agent will be able to negotiate an offer more effectively than you for a number of reasons.

● **Experience**. Your agent has the experience of having negotiated many other sales before.

● **Emotional involvement**. The agent should be able to negotiate in a calm and businesslike fashion without the burden of emotional involvement.

● **Extra thinking time**. Direct negotiations often mean that you are forced into giving an answer or making a concession on the spot. By negotiating through a third party, who does not have the authority to reach a binding agreement on your behalf, you buy invaluable thinking time.

An astute buyer will know that he will be better off by negotiating directly with you the vendor and may try to apply considerable pressure in an attempt to persuade you not to involve the agent in the negotiations. You should not give in to such tactics. Doing so could cost you thousands of pounds.

Don't take offence at low offers

Under the Estate Agents Act, an estate agent must inform you of every offer that he receives for your property immediately and in writing. Should you receive what you consider to be an insulting offer for your property, don't shoot the messenger. Your agent is only complying with his statutory duty.

The receipt of frequent low offers is also evidence that the agent is doing his job effectively by asking everyone who views the property if there is any price at which they would be interested in buying. This type of closing question does occasionally result in a sale to a purchaser who is embarrassed about making a low offer. Unfortunately, it also produces a number of low offers.

Do conduct negotiations in writing

Negotiations should be conducted in writing or by fax wherever possible. This will ensure that your position is not misrepresented and will save a lot of unnecessary arguments about exactly what was agreed later on.

ESTABLISHING IF THE BUYER CAN PROCEED

Before you even begin to discuss the issue of price, it is vital to find out about your potential buyer's ability to proceed. Vital questions to ask include:

● The buyer's ideal time-scale.

● The reason for the move.

● Has the buyer got property to sell?

● If so, has that property been sold?

● If so, what stage has the sale reached?

● Are there any other dependent transactions in the chain?

- If so, exactly what stage has each transaction reached?

- Will the buyer require a mortgage?

- If so, what percentage of the purchase price will the mortgage be for?

- Which mortgage lender does the buyer intend to use?

You should be extremely wary about dealing with any buyer who cannot or will not answer these essential questions.

WEIGHING UP THE OFFER

Whilst price will usually be the most important factor, speed and certainty will also be important to most sellers. An offer that is slow to complete could cost you an extra mortgage payment or might even result in you losing your purchase. You should also remember that an offer that falls through will, apart from the disappointment, also cost you a substantial amount of money in wasted legal and survey fees.

Factors that could prevent a buyer from completing his purchase quickly and smoothly might include:

- length of chain

- size of mortgage required

- choice of lending source

- choice of solicitor.

Length of chain
Every additional transaction in the chain increases the chances of something going wrong. You should be looking for someone with the shortest possible chain. Purchasers with nothing to sell are best of all.

Size of mortgage required
A buyer who has applied for a high percentage mortgage (say 95 per cent or more) may be unable to proceed if the property is downvalued on survey. Generally speaking buyers who need to borrow a lower percentage of the purchase price are more likely to complete. Cash buyers are the most likely to complete of all.

Choice of lending source

Some lending sources are able to get most mortgage offers out within days. Others take weeks. Ask your estate agent if he has an opinion about the efficiency of the lending source that your buyer has chosen.

Choice of solicitor

A solicitor who is inexperienced, pedantic, overworked or just inefficient can delay a sale for weeks. Ask your agent for his opinion of the firm that the buyer has chosen.

All these factors should be carefully weighed up before you decide on what price you would be prepared to accept from the buyer.

HANDLING AN OFFER FROM A BUYER UNABLE TO PROCEED

On many occasions your enquiries will reveal that your would-be buyer is not yet in a position to proceed. Common reasons would be:

- the buyer is unlikely to be able to raise the money

- the buyer has not yet found a buyer for his own property

- the buyer has an incomplete chain.

There are very few circumstances where you have anything to gain from giving a commitment to sell your property to someone who is not yet in a position to buy it and the best advice is usually to refuse to even commence negotiations until the buyer is able to proceed. You should be warned that people can get very emotional about losing a house that they have set their heart on and some may try to persuade you to accept their offer by making all sorts of rash promises. Do not be swayed, most will amount to nothing.

When refusing an offer from such a buyer, the greatest care must be taken to remain on good terms with him. His buying position can and often does change overnight and you must do everything possible to ensure that it is easy for him to come back to you if and when he sells his own property.

Sell the benefits of your position

A good buyer will be just as concerned as you to avoid the expense and disappointment of an abortive sale and the attractiveness of your position as a seller could well influence the price that the buyer is prepared

Dear Mr Jones,

Re: 27 The Avenue, Anytown. Subject to contract.

1. Thank you for your offer for the above property of £90,000.

2. I understand that your buying position is as follows:

● You have sold your existing property to a first time buyer.

● Your own buyers have a mortgage offer and are pushing you to find somewhere.

● You will be arranging a mortgage for approximately 70 per cent of the purchase price from the XYZ Building Society.

● You would like to exchange contracts in 6-8 weeks.

3. I confirm that I am not buying another property immediately and that I would be prepared to move out of the house within 6-8 weeks.

4. The price that I would be prepared to accept for the property is £97,000 and I believe that this is fully justified by the prices achieved for similar houses in the area. Relevant comparables include:

5. Number 37 which has no garage was recently sold for £95,000. Number 45 which is very similar to mine recently sold for £97,500.

6. I believe that both the house and my selling position could suit you and your family very well and we would like to sell to you if a price can be agreed.

I look forward to hearing from you with a revised offer shortly,

Yours sincerely

Fig. 4. Responding to an offer to purchase.

to pay. If you are in a good position to sell, you should be sure to point this out when responding to an offer. Circumstances that may be attractive to a buyer would include:

- ability to move out immediately or at short notice if necessary

- short upward chain

- not buying another property

- already found a property to buy.

NEGOTIATING THE PRICE

Your initial response should be in writing. It should follow this format:

(1) Thank the purchaser for his offer (regardless of how low it was).

(2) Summarise your understanding of the purchaser's buying position (this will help to avoid arguments later).

(3) Sell the benefits of your selling position.

(4) State the price that you would be prepared to accept.

(5) Give your detailed justification for how you arrived at this figure.

(6) Restate that you are keen to sell.

(7) Ask the buyer to make a revised offer.

Figure 4 shows an example of such a letter.

EMPLOYING NEGOTIATING TECHNIQUES

Few offers will be agreed in the first round. When conducting negotiations it is important to remember that both parties need to feel that they have won. If the other party is allowed to become entrenched in his position, it will become very much more difficult to achieve a satisfactory solution. There are many techniques that can be used to defuse the hostility of a negotiation.

Ask the purchaser to justify his offer

Almost every estate agent in the country can tell you a story about a sale that fell through because the two parties could not agree about the value of a garden shed, an old piece of carpet, a wooden toilet seat or something equally ridiculous.

The danger of conventional negotiation techniques is that they are highly confrontational. All too often such negotiations become deadlocked because both parties are too proud to concede another round. This is an emotional, not a rational, response but it could easily cost you a sale if you let it.

A much better way to negotiate is based on the simple principle of asking the other party to explain *how* he arrives at his offer. You might achieve this by writing a letter to him along the lines suggested in Figure 5.

Dear Mr Jones,

Re: 27 The Avenue, Anytown. Subject to contract.

Thank you for your revised offer of £95,000. In my last letter I showed you how I arrived at my figure of £97,000 by reference to two comparable properties in the immediate area. I wondered if you would be kind enough to let me know *how* you arrived at your figure of £95,000.

I do hope that we will be able to reach an agreement and I look forward to hearing from you again soon.

Yours sincerely

Fig. 5. Responding to a revised offer.

The buyer must respond with some sort of justification for the offer that he has made. This should ensure that future negotiations remain based on factual rather than emotional issues. This technique can be used again and again through subsequent rounds of the negotiations and can play an important role in preventing the negotiations from becoming deadlocked.

Trade concession for concession

It can be very dangerous to ask the other party to concede something without giving something in return. You should always be on the look-out for an opportunity to trade a concession for a concession. For example:

● If you will pay an extra £1,000 I will agree to take the property off the market immediately.

It is important to realise that the value of the concession need not be equal to the value of what you are asking for in return.

Offering non-financial concessions

A non-cash concession can often have a disproportionate value to the other party. For example, by moving out one day sooner you might be able to save your purchaser from paying a whole month's additional rent. It is therefore well worth trying to find out about any requirements of this nature that your buyer might have. These might include:

● completion date

● completion periods

● exchange date

● removal of the property from the market

● fixtures and fittings

● carpets and curtains.

By making concessions in these areas you might well be able to avoid deadlock and/or secure a valuable negotiating advantage.

Breaking deadlock

It is very frustrating to be unable to agree an offer for the sale of a relatively small amount of money. When the amount at stake is small it can be worth contacting some of the people higher up or down the chain to see if they are prepared to make a contribution. The vendor of a one million pound house at the top of the chain may be prepared to pay a few thousand pounds directly to someone lower down the chain in order to facilitate a move. It is usually best to leave it up to the agent to try to negotiate such a solution.

Always leave the door open

It is surprising how often purchasers who make a low offer for a property early in their search return to make an acceptable offer for the property days, weeks or even months later. For this reason it is vital to remain on good terms with everyone who makes an offer and to ensure that it is easy for them to reopen negotiations with you at any time in the future.

Consolidation

Once an offer has been agreed, it is important to ensure that all the details are confirmed in writing as soon as possible.

It is also worth trying to arrange to meet your potential purchaser again. A meeting after negotiations have been successfully concluded can play an important role in consolidating the sale. There is no doubt that sales where a personal relationship has been established between the vendor and the purchaser are much more likely to complete.

HANDLING MULTIPLE OFFERS

Occasionally a property will prove to be unexpectedly popular and two or more offers will be made by different purchasers within a short space of time. This can happen for a variety of reasons, one of which is that the property has been marketed at too low a price. If you suspect that this is the case review the comparable evidence before you go any further.

Multiple offers must be handled with great care. It is all too easy to start off with two or three offers and to end up with none. The purpose of this chapter is to help you to avoid this.

Look at the situation from the purchaser's point of view

Every potential purchaser who tries unsuccessfully to buy your property will be left with a bill for legal and survey fees of several hundred pounds. Each potential purchaser will therefore need to be reassured at the outset that he will be treated fairly and that he has a realistic chance of getting the property. If your behaviour during early negotiations does not achieve this, some or even all of your potential purchasers will withdraw.

Consider all the options

There are seven options for dealing with multiple offers:

1. A contract race

Two or more purchasers are told that whichever of them is able to exchange contracts on the property first will be allowed to buy it.

Advantages	–	no risk to vendor
	–	no need to choose between the parties
	–	more than one chance of selling
Disadvantages	–	even the suggestion of a contract race may cause both parties to withdraw
	–	losing party is left with legal fees to pay.

2. Race to mortgage offer

Two or more purchasers are told that whoever gets their written mortgage offer first will be allowed to buy the property.

Advantages	–	as above but abortive costs are lower to losing party
Disadvantages	–	successful party can still withdraw after mortgage offer received
	–	losing party must still bear some abortive costs
	–	may result in neither party proceeding.

3. Vendor funded contract race (or race to mortgage offer)

This works as in option 1. However, the vendor agrees to pay the legal and survey costs of whichever party loses up to an agreed figure.

Advantages	–	as option 1 but purchasers more likely to agree to participate if costs are underwritten
Disadvantages	–	reimbursement of legal fees cannot make up for the disappointment of losing a property
	–	suggestion of race may still frighten off both parties
	–	cost to vendor will be several hundred pounds.

4. Shut out agreement

A legal undertaking is given via the solicitors that one party will be given X weeks to exchange contracts without competition from any other buyer.

Advantages	–	seller is protected against a sale dragging on for an unreasonable period

Disadvantages   –   seller is forced to choose between potential buyers at the outset

                  –   seller gets no protection against buyer withdrawing.

5. Sealed bids
Buyers are invited to submit their best and final offer in writing. The sealed bids are opened at a pre-agreed time and the highest offer wins.

Advantages   –   buyers can become excited by a sealed bid contest and overpay

                  –   system is seen to be fair to all potential buyers

Disadvantages   –   system has no legal validity and has been discredited by previous unfair competitions in which the opening of the sealed bids has been followed by further rounds of negotiations

                  –   buyer who pays highest price may not be buyer who is most likely to proceed

                  –   a higher price might be obtained by open negotiations.

6. Open negotiations
The agent continues to negotiate with each buyer openly until all but one have dropped out of the bidding.

Advantages   –   often the best way to obtain the highest price

                  –   purchasers' buying positions can be taken into account

Disadvantages   –   negotiations can become acrimonious

                  –   successful buyer can withdraw at any time.

7. Remarketing the property
If you feel that the property has been undervalued the only option may be to remarket it. It will usually be necessary to leave a break of several weeks before the property is advertised again. You may also wish to change agents. This will cause considerable delays and when it is relaunched the initial impact will have been spoiled. For these reasons the decision to remarket a property should not be taken lightly.

Deciding which option is best for you

Different options or combinations of options will appeal in different circumstances. If you are selling a highly desirable property in a buoyant market, a contract race may be worth considering. If you are selling an unattractive property during a recession a shut out agreement might be more appropriate. Whatever option you finally choose I would urge you to remember three things:

1. Don't rush the decision.

2. Take your estate agent's advice.

3. Consider each buyer's position as well as the price offered.

CASE STUDY

Losing sight of what is reasonable

Neville received an offer of £220,000 for his luxury detached property which was for sale at £249,950. He responded quite aggressively and said that he would not take a penny less than £240,000. Over the next three days negotiations continued until all that was left between them was a garden shed. The buyer was determined to have it. Neville felt that he had already conceded so much that he could not bring himself to give in yet again. He eventually told the agent that he would rather burn the shed than let the buyer have it.

The agent offered to pay for a new shed out of his commission but it was too late – negotiations had broken down and the sale did not proceed.

CHECKLIST

● Always negotiate through a third party.

● Try to conduct negotiations in writing.

● Check that the buyer is able to proceed *before* accepting their offer.

● Ask the buyer to justify the price offered.

● Make full use of non-financial concessions such as completion dates and carpets.

● Always leave a door open for the future.

● Be very careful when dealing with multiple offers. It is all too easy to start with three offers and end up with none.

8
Getting the Sale through to Completion

EXAMINING THE KEY STAGES

Whilst almost everyone agrees that the English house buying system is thoroughly unsatisfactory, no one yet has been able to come up with an acceptable alternative. For the time being at least, it seems that we are stuck with a process that is cumbersome, outdated and so inefficient that something like one in three of all the sales that are agreed fail to complete. The purpose of this section is to help you to reduce the chances of suffering the expense and disappointment of an abortive sale.

Key steps in the process
The first step in preventing an abortive sale is to understand the process. This is explained in the flow chart in Figure 6.

How long will it take?
Some sales complete within seven days, a few have been known to complete within 24 hours. However, such instances are really quite rare. A more usual time-scale for a straightforward sale would be four to eight weeks for an exchange of contracts and a further four weeks for completion. A complicated sale could take several times as long as this.

The importance of regular progress chasing
Your sale will not complete within the usual time-scale unless you chase it. Some solicitors and mortgage lenders are like wheelbarrows. If you stop pushing you will come back to find that they are still exactly where you left them!

You and your agent need to work together to keep the pressure up. Unfortunately, some agents believe that once an offer has been accepted, their job is done. You must make it very clear to your agent that you will not stand for this. Tell him at the outset that you will expect him to speak to the purchaser, the lending source and both solicitors at least once a week until contracts are exchanged and to report back to you on a weekly basis with a detailed progress report.

Figure 6 shows a much simplified version of how things should happen. In practice a great many things can and do go wrong. Each of these stages will be explained in detail later in this section.

DECIDING WHEN TO TAKE THE PROPERTY OFF THE MARKET

Just because you have accepted an offer, there is nothing to say that you should not continue to market your property. Whether or not to actually do so can be a difficult decision to make. On the one hand you will wish to show your purchaser good faith. On the other you must remind yourself that a third of all sales don't complete. It may be helpful to delay a final decision on this until after you have done three things:

1. Double-checked the chain.

2. Got to know the purchaser.

3. Considered the available options.

Double-checking the chain

Sometimes in the rush to agree an offer, there is no time to check out the chain in as much detail as you would have liked. If this is the case then the time to get the rest of this background information is now. You cannot give your buyer a commitment to take the property off the market until you are absolutely sure that he is in a position to proceed.

Getting to know your purchasers

Consider asking the purchasers to visit you again at home as soon as negotiations have been finalised. The visit will give you an excellent opportunity to make a more accurate assessment of the extent to which you feel you can trust them. It will also give you a chance to get to know each other. The quality of the relationship formed between buyer and seller can be a very important factor in preventing unreasonable behaviour later on.

Considering the alternative options

There are many alternatives to the conventional option of an oral promise to take the property off the market. Each of the following may be appropriate in different circumstances:

A written lock out agreement

A very nervous buyer might ask you to sign a lock out agreement. This

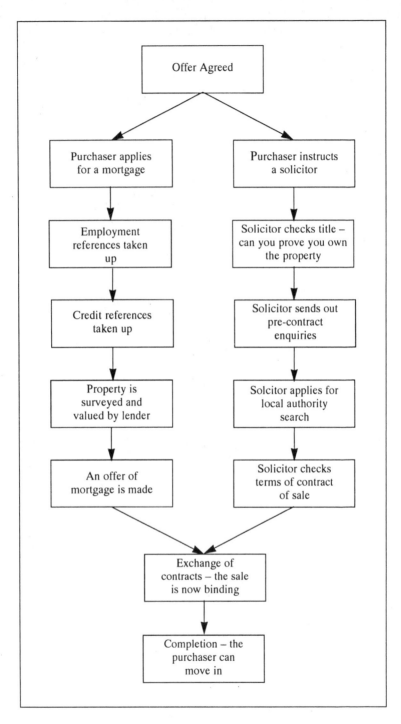

Fig. 6. The key steps in the sales process.

is a legal contract that prevents you from selling the property to any other party for a specified period (typically 7-28 days). Such an undertaking should only be given to a buyer who is in an excellent position to proceed and then only as a last resort.

A written or verbal agreement to take the property off the market for a given period (typically 7-28 days)
This gives the buyers a head start but leaves you the option to remarket the property at an early date if the buyer has not made satisfactory progress. Such an undertaking can give considerable comfort to a keen buyer who is in a position to proceed.

Left on market but not advertised
This gives the buyer very little comfort or protection. It may be appropriate in a buoyant market or when there are doubts about the buyer's ability to proceed.

Left on market with an assurance that second offers will not be accepted
The buyer is told that you are not seeking a better offer but that you cannot take the risk of taking the property off the market. This undertaking is virtually worthless and you must be sure that it will not deter a buyer from proceeding. It may be appropriate in a rising market, when you are unsure about the buyer or when you need to hurry the buyer to exchange contracts quickly.

Left on market, no promises
Many good buyers may be unwilling to spend money on survey fees and legal fees when there is no guarantee that they will be able to buy the house. Such a solution is usually only possible in a very buoyant market or with a buyer who is not in a position to proceed.

Whichever option you choose it is vital to keep your word once you have given it. A buyer who is told that a house has been taken off the market will be furious if he sees it advertised the following week. A great many sales fall through because the purchaser is given cause to believe that he cannot trust the vendor to keep his word.

CASE STUDY

Losing the buyer's goodwill

Stanley and Ethel agreed a sale on their house within a week of putting it onto the market. They got on well with their buyer and expected the sale to go through without difficulty but just to be on the safe side they decided to leave the property on the market in case anything went wrong. They did not mention this to their buyer.

The following week the buyer rang their agent in a fury. He said that he had just seen the house advertised in the paper – what did Stanley and Ethel think they were playing at? He was doing everything he could to proceed with the sale as quickly as possible. He feared they were trying to obtain a higher offer from another buyer. He said that if that was their attitude he would back out of the sale and buy from someone more trustworthy.

Stanley and Ethel were devastated. It had never been their intention to try to get a higher offer – they just wanted a safety net in case something went wrong.

The agent tried persuading their buyer but to no avail. The house was quickly sold to someone else for the same price but the whole episode left a bad taste and Stanley and Ethel still regret the fact that their buyer accused them unjustifiably of trying to gazump him. With hindsight they wish they had discussed the issue of leaving the property on the market at the very outset.

CHECKLIST

● Have you double-checked the chain?

● Have you discussed the issue of leaving the property on the market openly with your purchasers and/or your agent?

9
Dealing with the Legal Side

CHOOSING A SOLICITOR

The right solicitor will be able to help you to avoid a great many of the common legal problems. When choosing a solicitor there are several important points to bear in mind.

Choose a specialist

You need to choose a solicitor who specialises in residential conveyancing. This person is an expert in his field and will have come across all the common conveyancing problems before. This will help to ensure that your sale or purchase reaches a swift and trouble-free conclusion.

If you are using a small firm you should check to ensure that they deal with conveyancing on a regular basis. It is perfectly in order to ask them over the telephone how many conveyances they have dealt with during the last year.

Instruct one solicitor, not two

If you are buying a property, the second thing to check is that the solicitor that you have in mind is 'on the panel' (*ie* has been approved by your mortgage lender). In most cases the purchaser's solicitor will act for both the purchaser and the mortgage lender. However, if your solicitor is not on your mortgage lender's panel, they will insist on instructing a second solicitor to check your solicitor's work and safeguard their interests. This will inevitably mean unnecessary expense and delay. The question to ask before you instruct your solicitor is 'I will be obtaining a mortgage from the XYZ Building Society, are you on their panel?' If the answer is no, find another solicitor.

Don't choose on price alone

Most solicitors these days will be prepared to give a free quotation over the telephone. You will find however that conveyancing quotations vary enormously – a variation of 100 per cent or more would not be uncommon. While price is an important factor, it is very important not to select a solicitor on price alone. If a firm quotes a fee that is significantly below that of their competitors, then they will cut corners in their service somewhere in order to make a profit. In practice, this might mean that most of the actual work is done by an unqualified clerk rather than a partner, or that less time overall will be spent on each case. This might mean that your solicitor does not have time to answer telephone enquiries. The delays and frustration that can be caused by an overworked or inefficient solicitor will far outweigh the saving in the conveyancing fee.

Get a recommendation

The best way to choose a solicitor is by recommendation. Ask your estate agent, friends and neighbours who have moved recently and your mortgage lender or broker for a recommendation. You will often find that the same firm is mentioned several times.

When to instruct a solicitor

If you are selling a property there is a great deal to be said for instructing a solicitor when you put the property onto the market rather than waiting until you have found a buyer. This will enable your solicitor to do some of the preparatory work such as obtaining the deeds in advance. This can save a lot of time once a buyer has been found.

Handling your own conveyancing

It is perfectly possible to handle your own conveyancing. Several step by step DIY conveyancing guides have been published and the work involved is not actually all that time consuming or complicated. However, the reaction of everyone else involved in the transaction – the estate agent, the other solicitor, the lending source, and your purchaser or vendor – will be 'Oh no, they're not doing their own conveyancing, are they?'

This hostile attitude can, on its own, cause considerable delays and my advice to most people therefore would be to leave conveyancing to the professionals.

OVERCOMING LEGAL PROBLEMS

The things that can go wrong with a sale are almost innumerable and it would be impossible to cover them all in a single chapter. However, in my experience there are some problems that seem to come up time and time again. These include:

● lost title deeds

- disputes over the title

- delay in producing the draft contract

- lost contract

- delay in obtaining office copy entries on a land register

- restrictive covenants

- a caution

- solicitor's enquiries before contract

- delays with local authority searches

- building regulation infringements

- disputes over fixtures and fittings

- arguments over the deposit

- use of deposit by vendor

- dispute over completion dates.

Lost title deeds

The title deeds prove that you own your property. If the property is mortgaged they will almost certainly be held by your mortgage lender. If you own your property outright, the title deeds may be held by the solicitor who acted for you when you bought your property, by your bank or by a previous mortgage lender. On the other hand, they could have slipped down behind the radiator or have been thrown away by accident. If the title deeds to your property have been mislaid, you will need to prove again that you actually own the property. This may cause a considerable delay.

If you are selling a property, the best way to avoid such delays is to ask your solicitor to obtain the deeds at the time that you put your property onto the market, rather than waiting until a sale has been agreed.

Disputes over the title

There are two systems of land conveyancing in England and Wales. In the registered system the title to the land is registered at the land registry and is guaranteed by the state. Disputes over title are therefore rare. In the unregistered system the title is not registered at all and must be proved by checking the details of previous conveyances.

Where land is unregistered disputes over title are more common and negotiations can become quite protracted. One day all land will be registered. In the meanwhile if you find that the property that you are buying or selling is unregistered you should be prepared to allow extra time for the conveyancing process to be completed.

If you are selling a property, the best way to minimise any delay is again to instruct a solicitor at the time that you put the property onto the market.

Delay in producing the draft contract

These days most draft contracts are completed largely of standard or semi-standard phrases stored on a word processor. Unless there is something highly unusual about the property that is being sold, any delay in producing a draft contract is most likely to be caused by the inefficiency of the vendor's solicitors.

Lost contract

If a contract is lost, a copy can usually be produced within minutes on a word processor. A lost contract should therefore not be accepted as a reason for a delay.

Delay in obtaining office copy entries

Proof of title is supported by a copy, officially prepared by the land registry, of the entries on a land register. An office copy entry is divided into three sections: Section A confirms the address of the property, Section B confirms the quality of the title and Section C lists any charges or restrictive covenants.

The land registry is usually quite efficient and can be expected to provide office copy entries within seven to ten working days. The most common reason for delay is that the solicitor has not made an application for office copy entries soon enough.

Restrictive covenants

A restrictive covenant is a promise not to use a property for certain specified purposes. Common examples would include:

● not to use a property for any trade or business

- to keep the fences in good repair

- not to build another house on the plot.

Restrictive covenants can cause enormous problems and often cause delays in a sale.

The problems that covenants cause fall into two categories. In some cases, the existing property is in breach of an old covenant (*eg* a house has been converted into flats). In other cases the prospective purchaser wishes to do something that would break a covenant (*eg* build an extension or work from home).

Problems with covenants can be resolved in two ways. The first option us to track down the holder of the covenant and persuade him, or pay him, to release the property from it. However, in many cases this is not possible because his current address is not known or perhaps because he has long since died.

The alternative is to buy an insurance policy that covers the new owner against any loss that would be suffered in the event that the covenant is ever enforced. In most cases this is the quicker way to solve the problem.

A caution

A caution is a warning placed on the Charges Register by a person who believes that he has an interest in a property which is not recorded. The most common caution would be placed by an estranged husband or wife who did not buy a property in joint names, but who still has an interest in it. The process for removing a caution involves writing to the Registrar. The Registrar has wide discretion to do what he thinks is appropriate. It may involve the payment of a sum of money to the person named in the caution or it may even involve a court case. The process of removing a caution can be quite protracted and may cause severe delays.

Enquiries before contract

This is a list of questions sent by the purchaser's solicitor to the vendor's solicitor. The list is quite long and can appear daunting. However, in practice most of the questions are standard and many of the answers are 'I do not know' or 'rely on your own enquiries'.

Some questions do seem to cause a disproportionate number of problems, particularly:

- arguments about boundaries and fences

- arguments about sewers and drains

- arguments about access roads and rights of way.

Very often the best way to resolve such issues is to visit the property and discuss the problem directly with the other party. Frequently a problem that could not be resolved in an exchange of three or four letters can be sorted out in five minutes face to face.

Delays with local authority searches

The local authority search confirms amongst other things that the property has complied with all current building regulations, that no new property is to be built within 50 yards, and that no major road scheme is contemplated within 200 yards. The mortgagor will not allow contracts to be exchanged until these enquiries have been answered. Unfortunately many local authorities have a considerable backlog of enquiries to deal with and a delay of up to two or three months is not uncommon in some areas. There are three ways to prevent a delay in obtaining a search from holding up your sale:

1. The best solution is to ask your solicitor to apply for a local authority search immediately your property is put onto the market. The downside is that the search could be out of date by the time a sale has been agreed.

2. If a sale has previously fallen through, another solution may be to try to buy the search from the solicitors who acted for the purchaser who did not proceed.

3. The final option is to do a personal search. You can literally do this yourself but most people retain a professional company to undertake the search on their behalf. If a mortgage is involved it will often be necessary to buy an insurance policy to warranty the purchaser against anything that has been missed by the person who undertook the search.

Building regulation infringements

Many sales run into problems because an extension or other alteration has been completed without building regulation approval. In some cases it is possible to persuade the council to issue a certificate retrospectively. However, the council may wish to make fairly extensive checks on the property before they are prepared to do this. In extreme cases it has proved impossible to sell a property until the offending alteration has been removed or demolished.

Disputes over fixtures and fittings

The issue of which fixtures and fittings are to be included in the sale is one that often arouses considerable passions. The best way to ensure that such disputes do not hinder or jeopardise your sale is to ensure that a detailed list of fixtures and fittings is recorded in writing and agreed at the time that the offer is accepted.

Arguments over the deposit

Many solicitors advise their clients to accept a minimum deposit of ten per cent. This can cause real problems if the purchaser is applying for a 95 or 100 per cent mortgage. The main purpose of a deposit is to cover the vendor against any loss that he might incur in the event that the sale does not complete. Bearing in mind how rare it is for a sale to fall through between exchange of contracts and completion, you may decide to accept a reduced deposit of say 5 per cent. The alternative is for the purchasers to borrow the money from their bank, who may require a solicitor's undertaking to repay the loan once the mortgage funds have been released. It is as well to clarify your solicitor's attitude to this before the problem arises.

Use of deposit by vendor

You may want to use your purchaser's ten per cent deposit to fund the deposit that is required from your own vendor. Some solicitors have strong views about this and will not allow their client's deposit monies to be used in this way. It is therefore well worth establishing at an early stage whether you will be allowed to use your purchaser's deposit to fund your own purchase. If not, you will need a loan for this amount from your bank, who may require an undertaking from your own solicitor to repay it from the proceeds of your sale.

Dispute over completion dates

A completion date is usually set for 28 days after exchange of contracts. However, completion periods can be shortened to a few days; indeed it is even possible to do a simultaneous exchange and completion. Conversely the completion period can be lengthened. In some cases completions have been set for more than a year after exchange of contracts.

The more people there are involved in a chain the more difficult it is to find a completion date that is satisfactory to all parties. Again this is an issue that should be discussed in advance in order to avoid last minute problems.

EXAMINING LEASEHOLD PROPERTIES

Short lease
Many mortgage lenders will not lend on property where the lease has less than 50 years left to run. Many purchasers therefore are reluctant to buy a property with a lease of less than 60 years. Where a lease is shorter than this, it will often be necessary to negotiate a lease extension with the freeholder. This will almost certainly involve the payment of a fairly substantial sum of money and negotiations can become quite protracted. If you own a property with a lease of less than 60 years it is well worth making initial enquiries of your landlord about the cost of a lease extension at the time that you first put your property onto the market.

Defects with the lease
The purchaser's solicitor may claim to have found a defect in your lease. Sometimes the explanation is that the purchaser's solicitor is being pedantic. Sometimes the defect will be relatively minor and can be resolved through negotiation. On other occasions the defect will prove to be more serious. Some of the leases that were drawn up for the flats converted from large houses during the property boom of the 1980s were very carelessly worded. One of the worst examples that I heard of involved the owner of a first floor flat who did not have the right to walk from the road to his own front door. This was because the solicitor who drew up the lease had forgotten to give him the right to walk across a front garden that belonged to the ground floor flat.

Where a defect in the lease is serious, it will need to be corrected by a Deed of Variation. This needs the freeholder's approval. The freeholder will almost certainly require that you bear the legal costs associated with drawing up a Deed of Variation and most freeholders will also require a payment for their inconvenience. Negotiations over a Deed of Variation can become quite protracted and the costs involved can be substantial. Where a defect in the lease is very serious, you may have a claim for negligence against the solicitor who handled the conveyancing for you when you bought the property.

Unpaid service charges
Leasehold sales are often delayed because the vendor owes service charges to his freeholder. Even if such charges are in dispute, it will usually be necessary to pay them before contracts can be exchanged.

CASE STUDY

Getting what you pay for

First time buyers Benjamin and Samantha obtained conveyancing quotes that ranged from £99 to nearly £500 plus disbursements plus VAT for the purchase of a one bedroom converted flat in a large Victorian house. They instructed the cheapest solicitor and had problems throughout their purchase. The first problem was that the solicitor whom they had originally spoken to was never available. The work was done by an unqualified assistant whom they had very little confidence in and even he was seldom available.

The purchase itself was dogged by one problem after another. There was a defect with the lease, there was a dispute with the local council, who said that some of the work that had been done to the property did not meet building regulations and the service charges hadn't been paid for many years. To make matters worse when the purchase eventually completed they received a legal bill of nearly £500 for all the extra work involved. With hindsight they wish that they had chosen their solicitor with greater care.

10
Understanding the Survey Process

KNOWING WHAT TO DO WHEN THE SURVEY IS LATE

Often the first sign that a sale is not proceeding properly is a delay in arranging a survey appointment. Where the purchasers are seeking a mortgage, a survey will usually be arranged within two to three weeks of the offer being accepted. Where the purchasers are buying for cash, a structural survey should usually be arranged within one to two weeks. If a survey is not booked within these time-scales then you need to find out why.

Encountering problems with references

A surprisingly high proportion of perfectly creditworthy people are refused a mortgage because they do not meet the mortgagor's strict lending criteria. Common problems involve:

● credit scoring

● overtime and bonus payments

● employer's reference

● county court judgements for debt.

Credit scoring

Many lenders use a credit scoring process. This means that potential borrowers are given plus marks for some aspects of their lifestyle, for example being married with a family, and minus marks for others, such as having changed their job too frequently.

Whilst it may be statistically true that married borrowers are less likely to default on their mortgage payments, the credit scoring process is extremely arbitrary and if often leads to perfectly reputable and creditworthy applicants being refused a loan.

Overtime and bonus payments

Many lenders will only allow half the value of overtime and bonus payments when calculating how much they will lend. Thus a civil servant on £20,00 pa could borrow £60,000, while a salesman on £10,000 pa basic plus £10,000 commission could only borrow £45,000. This can cause great confusion and delay. The problem can sometimes be overcome if the purchaser's employer will confirm in writing that the bonus payments are guaranteed, or if other evidence is available (such as bank statements) to show that the bonuses have been paid for a long time (say more than two years).

Employer's reference
The lender will usually require a written reference from the borrower's employer. Employers are often very slow to comply with such requests. It is the purchaser's job to chase his employer to ensure that the mortgage application is not held up due to this.

County court judgments for debt
A great many mortgage applications are refused because a routine credit search reveals that the borrower has a county court judgment (CCJ) for debt registered against him. Often a CCJ is evidence that a borrower is a bad credit risk, but in many instances it is evidence only of the rottenness of the system under which CCJs are recorded.

Anyone can seek to obtain a CCJ against anyone else by filling out a form which will be sent to the defendant's last known address. Many thousands of innocent people have CCJs registered against them because they did not know how to defend the action, or because the papers were sent to a previous address.

A further problem is that the search will include all CCJs registered at a given address, not just those recorded against the borrower personally. This means that credit is often denied because of a CCJ registered against an adult son or daughter, a divorced spouse, even a lodger who is living, or has previously lived, at the same address.

Despite the inadequacies of the present system, lenders will take the discovery of an undeclared CCJ extremely seriously and it will nearly always result in the mortgage application being refused.

Dealing with these problems
Whilst problems with references will undoubtedly delay the progress of your sale, they need not prevent your buyer from proceeding. Many problems can be resolved by negotiation with the lender. Even if the first mortgage application is refused point blank, there is a good chance that a new application will be accepted by an alternative lender.

You can, however, only help to solve problems that you know about. Many purchasers are so embarrassed at being refused a mortgage that they tell the agent that they have changed their mind about buying the house without saying why. In such circumstances you are absolutely dependent on the skill and persistence of your agent to uncover the real reason for their change of heart, and if appropriate, to persuade the purchasers to reapply to an alternative lending source.

Coping with an inefficient lender

Sometimes the reason for the delay is just sheer inefficiency on behalf of the lender. Lending sources vary enormously in the time that it takes to turn round a straightforward mortgage application. Some are notoriously inefficient – your agent will know which they are. The only solution is to get your purchaser to chase his lender more frequently – every day if necessary – until the required action is taken. In the most extreme case you might try to persuade the purchaser to withdraw his application and reapply to a more efficient lender.

Coping with delays caused by the surveyor

Sometimes your enquiries will reveal that the delay in carrying out the survey is the fault of the surveyor. Perhaps the surveyor is on holiday or in the middle of a particularly busy spell.

If you suspect this is the case you should ask the purchaser or the agent to ring the surveyor to ask either for a firm date for a survey or for the return of the papers.

Understanding the survey options

Your purchaser will almost certainly commission one of three types of survey:

Mortgage valuation survey
This is the least comprehensive type of survey available. A typical report would be about two pages long. The purpose of this type of survey is to ensure that the property is satisfactory security for the mortgage that is advanced.

Home buyer's report
This is a much more comprehensive survey. It is intended to give the buyer a good idea about the condition of the property being purchased. It is prepared in a standard format in order to keep costs down. It will typically cost about twice as much as the mortgage valuation.

Full structural survey
This is the most comprehensive type of survey. It is prepared from scratch and will go into much more detail than the house buyer's report. It will typically cost about four times as much as the mortgage valuation.

It is clearly in your best interests to try to ensure that your property is surveyed in the least possible detail. The best way to achieve this is to have available your own recent structural survey. However, if a full structural survey is to take place you should try to ensure that it is combined with the mortgage valuation. Some buyers commission a basic mortgage valuation in the first instance then, once they have the result of this, commission a full structural survey. This is a more expensive way of doing things for the purchaser. Furthermore it can lead to unnecessary delays between the two survey reports.

AVOIDING A DOWN VALUATION

A great many sales fall through because the building society valuer down values the property on survey.

Why does it happen?
The valuer is retained by the mortgage lender and his role is to ensure that the property is satisfactory security for the size of the loan that is to be advanced. Because he is retained by the lender, the surveyor will err on the side of caution when valuing a property. The consequence is that the mortgage valuation can often be five or ten per cent less than the sale price that has been agreed.

What can be done to avoid the problem?
The best way to avoid the problems caused by a down valuation is to prevent it from happening in the first place. There is a great deal that you can do to achieve this:

Choosing the lending source
Some banks and building societies have a reputation for using over-cautious valuers. Your estate agent will know which they are, locally. If your purchaser is intending to apply to one of these lending sources, you should ask your agent to try to dissuade them. The best way to do so is by telling them the true reasons for your concerns. If the property is down valued your buyer will lose his survey fee and have to find another property. He should be as keen to avoid a down valuation as you and he will often be prepared to reconsider his choice of lending source in order to do so.

Choosing the surveyor
Some building societies employ their own full-time salaried valuers, but
most still instruct an independent local surveyor. Each local surveyor
will take a different view of property values and most towns have at least
one who has a reputation for down valuing. Your goal must be to prevent this surveyor from valuing your property. Your agent should be able
to help you to achieve this by asking the purchaser or his mortgage broker to telephone the building society to request that the particular surveyor is not instructed. They will often comply with such a request.

Preparing the house for the survey appointment
Surveyors are human too, and a well presented house will often be valued at a higher price than un untidy one. You should prepare for the surveyor's appointment in exactly the same way as you would prepare for
any other viewing.

Showing the house to best advantage
The surveyor should be shown round the house in exactly the same way
as any other purchaser. First impressions count for a lot and a local surveyor will probably have decided what value to put on the property
within a few minutes of arrival.

Once you have shown the surveyor quickly around the house he will
wish to be left alone to complete his detailed report. This might take
anywhere between 30 minutes and four hours depending on the size of
the property and the type of the report that is being prepared.

Providing comparable evidence
The surveyor will value your property on the basis of the evidence of
prices achieved for similar properties. One of the best ways to protect
against a down valuation is to give the surveyor your own selection of
property particulars, chosen to support the sale price achieved for your
property. This must be done tactfully. The surveyor will not respond
well if he thinks that you are trying to tell him how to do his job.

Handling a down valuation

Whatever precautions you take, there is still a very good chance that
your property will be down valued by the surveyor. We will look next at
what can be done to limit the damage.

Getting in first
Your estate agent will often be able to find out what figure the property
has been valued at a day or two before the purchaser is told. This

advance warning will enable the agent to present the bad news to the purchasers himself in the right way and can be an important factor in helping him to save the sale.

The initial response
Most buyers will use a surveyor's down valuation as an excuse to renegotiate the purchase price. You will wish to do everything possible to avoid this happening.

Your first response should be to defend your position. You might try three arguments:

1. Explain that the surveyor's job is to act on behalf of the mortgage lender and that the valuation is therefore bound to be a cautious one.

2. Point out that properties are often down valued on survey. Ask your agent to back this up with some statistics.

3. Remind the purchaser of the comparable evidence of other properties sold in the area which you used to justify the sale price that was agreed.

Subsequent negotiations
The key principles are:

●   negotiate via the agent

●   negotiate in writing

●   use positional bargaining techniques to avoid deadlock.

Ask the purchaser to justify his revised offer.

What to do if negotiations become deadlocked
If agreement cannot be reached your buyer will walk away. Before you allow this to happen you must pause to consider whether, taking all factors into account, this will be in your best interests. Factors to consider might include:

●   abortive legal costs

●   wasted survey costs on your purchase

- loss of interest on the proceeds, if moving down market or not buy-ing again

- chances of obtaining same purchase price from another buyer

- non-financial factors such as disappointment over the loss of your purchase.

Taking all these factors into account you will often find that the best course of action is to grit your teeth and accept the revised offer.

DEALING WITH REQUESTS FOR REPAIRS

As well as valuing cautiously, surveyors tend to take a pessimistic view about the extent and cost of any work that needs to be done to the prop-erty. The techniques outlined at the beginning of the last chapter will help to minimise such problems, but you must accept that the survey is likely to reveal at least one or two problems with the majority of properties.

The purchaser's likely response

The purchaser is likely to seize upon any problem revealed by the sur-vey as an opportunity to renegotiate the purchase price. His opening position is likely to be that the full cost of the repairs should be deduct-ed from the purchase price. You will need to work hard to defend your position.

Ask to see the survey report

Before you commence negotiations you should ask for a copy of the sur-vey report. It is in your purchaser's interests to exaggerate the cost and extent of the works that are deemed necessary and purchasers have even been known to invent problems not mentioned by the surveyor in order to try to get a price reduction. You should be very suspicious of a buyer who will not let you see the report. My instinctive reaction would be to refuse to commence negotiations without first seeing a copy of the survey report.

Interpreting the surveyor's report

Depending upon the urgency of the work, a surveyor will make one of the following recommendations:

- He can point out the fault and *recommend* that it is attended to.

● He can ask for a *formal undertaking* from the purchasers to carry out the necessary repairs within a certain time.

● He can insist that an *expert* is called in to investigate the extent of the problem and to assess the likely cost of rectifying it.

● He can recommend that the mortgage advance be made subject to a *retention*, that is to say that £X000 will be deducted from the mortgage advance and not released until the necessary work has been completed.

● He can recommend that the mortgage should be refused altogether.

Your initial response

Your initial response should be to refuse to renegotiate the price. You might try to defend your position using some of the following arguments:

● The surveyor has been pedantic – the work is not necessary at all.

● The work is of a cosmetic nature. The purchaser did not need a surveyor to point out that the kitchen and bathroom need updating and that the property is in need of redecoration.

● The condition of the property has already been allowed for in the price agreed.

● The other properties recently sold in the area were in a comparable condition.

● The defects mentioned must be seen as fair wear and tear in a property of this age.

Limiting the damage

If renegotiation seems inevitable, there is quite a lot that you can do to limit the damage.

Get your own estimate

The surveyor's estimate of the cost of necessary work is likely to be at the top end of the scale. It can be well worth asking a contractor to give an accurate estimate of the cost involved. It could prove to be a lot less than the surveyor thinks.

Offer to carry out the work yourself
Very often the buyer has absolutely no intention of carrying out the work
that his surveyor has recommended. He is just using the report to get a
price reduction. If you suspect that this is the case, you might counter it
by offering to do the work yourself between exchange of contracts and
completion.

Offer a proportion of the cost
If the sale were to fall through at this stage, both parties would stand to
lose a great deal. Having got so far, your buyer will wish to complete the
purchase if at all possible and may well be prepared to settle for a price
concession that represents only a small percentage of the cost of the
works.

Dealing with a very adverse survey
A very adverse survey report would be defined as one where the
mortgage advance is refused altogether or where a mortgage offer is
made subject to a retention of more than 20 per cent of the property's
value. By far the most common reason for such a result is **subsidence**.

It is unlikely that you will be able to negotiate your way out of a situation like this and it is almost inevitable that you will lose your purchaser and experience considerable delays before the property can be
sold again.

The action you take might include:

● **Commissioning your own structural survey**. Just occasionally a
   second surveyor will not consider the problem to be serious.

● **Commissioning a specialist structural engineer's report**.
   Surveyors have a tendency to spot a crack and assume that a property is about to fall down. A structural engineer's report might
   prove that the problem is not as severe as it looks.

● **Make an insurance claim**. The cost of rectifying such serious
   defects will usually be covered by your buildings insurance.

Don't panic
If negotiations reach deadlock, the best advice would be don't panic and
don't give the property away. It is surprising how often a second survey
reveals none of the problems mentioned in the first.

CASE STUDY

Getting a second opinion

Aaron and Dorothy agreed a sale of their Victorian property at a figure of £120,000. Their buyer's surveyor found a number of defects with the property including 'a roof that would need replacing within five years' and faults with the damp course. The surveyor said in this condition the property was worth only £105,000.

Aaron and Dorothy were not prepared to sell at this price and the buyer withdrew. A second sale was agreed, also at £120,000, and a second survey arranged with a different surveyor. The problems with the damp course came up again but the roof was not mentioned and this time the surveyor's valuation was £115,000.

Aaron and Dorothy obtained an estimate that showed that the cost of rectifying the damp course was less than the surveyors had estimated and on this basis the sale went through at a price of £117,000.

Commenting on their experience, Aaron said 'I'm so glad we didn't sell to the first buyer at £105,000. It just shows that surveyors' opinions and valuations can vary considerably.'

CHECKLIST

● Prepare thoroughly for the surveyor's appointment and ensure that the property looks its best.

● Try to have available particulars of other properties that have been sold in the area to give the surveyor when he calls.

● Get the builder's quote before you commence negotiations over repairs.

● Try to handle all subsequent negotiations in writing and via a third party.

11
Troubleshooting

GAZUMPING

The practice of gazumping arouses fierce passions. It happens when the vendor agrees a sale for his property and then subsequently accepts a higher offer from another party. It can happen at any time during the sales process, from five minutes after the first offer was accepted right up to the day that exchange of contracts was due to take place.

Whose fault is it?

Gazumping is caused by human greed, not by estate agents. An estate agent's professional and legal duty is to carry out the instructions of his client. If his client instructs him to continue marketing a property after an offer has been accepted, then he must do so. If a second offer is subsequently received, it is the agent's legal duty to pass the offer on to the vendor. It is entirely up to the vendor to decide whether to accept or refuse the higher price.

What you must do before you decide

If you receive a higher offer after you have agreed a sale, you need to proceed very carefully. It is all too easy to start with two offers and end up with none at all.

Checking out the second buyer's position
Before you do anything you must check out that the second buyer is in a position to proceed. Having checked out his position, compare it with the current position of your original buyer. At one extreme there would be nothing to gain from accepting an offer than was only marginally higher from a purchaser who has not yet sold his own property. At the other extreme it would be much harder to turn down a higher offer from a cash buyer the day after your original purchaser has lost the buyer for his own property.

Assessing the value of all other factors
You must also be sure to weigh up the value of all other relevant factors in the equation. These might include:

- **Time-scale**. How quickly could the second purchaser complete? Would this delay cost you money (*eg* in extra mortgage payments)?

- **Fairness of price**. Is your property really worth the high price? If it is not the second sale may well not complete due to a downvaluation on survey.

- **Risk of losing your purchase**. Would the delay caused by switching buyers jeopardise your own purchase?

Considering all the options
There are many alternative ways in which you can use a second offer to your advantage. The options include:

- Accepting the second offer and telling the original buyer they have lost the property.

- Informing the original buyers that you have received a higher offer from another party and inviting them to match it. (This might go more than one round before a new price is finally agreed.)

- Inviting both parties to compete in a contract race for the property (benefit: quicker completion).

- Informing the original buyers that you have received a second offer. Tell them that you will not accept it provided that they exchange contracts before a certain date (benefit: quicker completion).

- Informing the original buyer that you have received a second offer which you will not accept because you have agreed to sell it to them (benefit: consolidates relationship with original buyer but implies that completion is on the horizon).

- Refusing second offer without telling the original buyer that you received one (this is sometimes the best way to deal with a nervous buyer).

Considering the moral and ethical implications

This section would not be complete without a few words about the effects of gazumping on the purchaser. If you do accept a second offer, the original buyers will be left with a substantial bill for abortive survey fees and legal costs in addition to the disappointment of having lost the property that they had set their hearts on. It is not my place to attempt to define the limits of moral behaviour, but I would ask that you should at least pause to consider the consequences of your actions before you make your final decision.

GAZUNDERING

When the market is poor gazundering is a common problem. A vendor is 'gazundered' when the buyer reduces his offer, without good reason, shortly before exchange of contract is due to take place.

The buyer who tries this tactic is banking on the fact that the financial and emotional costs to you of pulling out of the sale at such a late stage will exceed the value of the reduction that he has asked for. When the property market is poor, buyers often get away with it.

Limiting the damage

The following suggestions will help you to limit the damage if your purchaser tries to gazunder you.

Negotiate via the agent

You will probably be very angry with the buyer for trying to gazunder you and this anger will seriously reduce your ability to negotiate effectively. Further negotiations really must therefore be conducted via the estate agent.

Ask for reasons

Ask the buyer why he has reduced his offer at such a late stage. The buyer's embarrassment about the situation will be increased if he is forced to admit that he has no reason to ask for a price reduction and that he's trying it on.

Rejustify the price

Use comparable evidence to justify that the property is worth the original price that was agreed.

Making the final decision

If these tactics don't work you will be forced to make a decision about whether to accept the reduced offer. It is all too easy to allow anger and emotion to get in the way of making the right decision. Before you tell your purchaser to go to hell, be sure to weigh up the financial value of factors such as:

- extra mortgage payments while the property is remarketed

- the financial and emotional cost of losing your purchase

- your realistic chances of obtaining the same price again from another purchaser.

If you have a reserve buyer waiting in the wings you might be in a position to call your purchaser's bluff, but on many other occasions the best thing to do is to bite your lip and accept the lower offer.

Dealing with the consequences
There are two things that you might do to claw back some of the money that you have had to concede to your purchaser:

Gazunder your own vendor
Telephone the agent that you are buying through, explain that you have been gazundered and say that you fear that you will not now be able to complete your purchase at the original price agreed. This is a high-risk strategy. You may lose your purchase altogether, but if market conditions are so bad that you felt compelled to accept a lower offer, then your vendor might be forced to do the same.

Remove fixtures and fittings
If all else has failed you might consider getting your own back by removing all fixtures and fittings not included in the contract. These might include things such as extra security locks, bathroom fitments, shelves, light fittings, plants, *etc*. The collective value of these fittings can often run to many hundreds or even thousands of pounds.

KNOWING WHAT TO DO IF THE BUYER WITHDRAWS

Try to establish the reason
My experience is that once a buyer says that he wishes to withdraw from the purchase he usually does so. However, before you completely give up on your purchaser, it is worth double-checking to make sure that you know the real reason for his change of heart. It is surprisingly common

to find that there are problems that you don't know about which might be avoidable. For example your buyer might have been refused a mortgage and be too embarrassed to tell the agent this. Instead he just says that he has changed his mind. If the agent can find out the truth, he might be able to help him to obtain a loan from another lending source.

Don't despair
However disappointed you are, try not to despair. Your property sold once and it will sell again, you just need to be patient.

Don't proceed with your purchase
Unless you are extremely wealthy, you should not even think about continuing with your purchase until you have found a buyer for your own property. One of the saddest cases that I dealt with as an agent involved a family who took out a ruinously expensive bridging loan to buy their dream home, failed to sell their previous home and ended up having both repossessed by the mortgage lenders. It could easily happen to you. However perfect your dream home, there will always be another.

DEALING WITH CHAINS

All the problems covered in this third section can also occur with other sales up or down the chain. If you suspect that your own sale is being jeopardised or delayed by the inexperience or pigheadedness of other buyers and sellers in the chain, you may need to take matters into your own hands.

Establishing what the problem is
It can be surprisingly difficult to find out the real cause of the delay. As in the game of Chinese whispers, information tends to be distorted when it is passed through the many parties involved in the chain. Furthermore, once tempers have become frayed, many parties seem to become more interested in whose fault it is that the chain is being held up, than in finding a way in which the problem can be resolved. You will need to work hard to cut through such nonsense.

Start with your estate agent
It is your agent's job to know what is happening up and down the chain and he should certainly have an opinion as to what is causing the delay. However, no matter how convincing his explanation sounds, don't take his word for it. Ask him to contact all the other agents up and down the

chain in order to establish the up-to-date position with each sale from first-hand sources.

Checking a chain via the solicitors

If you are still not satisfied with the answers you are getting, a second option is to try to track the sale through the solicitors. Conveyancing solicitors habitually blame the other side for all delays, so ignore any such allegations and concentrate your questions on establishing where the problems lie and whether there is anything that you can do to expedite matters.

Start by asking your solicitor for his opinion as to where the problem lies. You might then consider checking this by phoning some or all of the solicitors in the chain. They are under no obligation to talk to you, and some will refuse to do so, but most will give you five minutes at least which should be ample time for you to achieve your purpose.

Checking discreetly with other vendors

A final option is to try to speak directly to all the other parties in the chain. Each vendor will almost certainly be able to give you a telephone number for his own purchaser and in this way it should be possible for you to speak personally to everyone involved.

You will probably be surprised by the number of contradictory stories that you hear from different parties. The only safe way to be sure that you have established the real problem is to obtain information from several different sources so that you may cross check its accuracy.

Late survey/mortgage denied

If a buyer further down the chain is having problems obtaining a mortgage then there is a great deal that you might be able to do to help. Better still send them a copy of this book open at the relevant page!

Inefficient solicitors

A less informed buyer in the chain might have instructed a solicitor who is inexperienced, overworked, lazy, pedantic, or just downright bloody-minded.

The best person to help you to overcome the shortcomings of another solicitor in the chain is your own solicitor. If you are faced with this situation you should ring your solicitor and share your concerns with him. In return for payment for the extra time involved he might be able to guide, cajole or bully the other solicitor into doing the job that he is being paid for.

Down valuation on survey or gazundering

The recommendations made in the last chapter may help to defuse the situation. If negotiations have already reached deadlock you might consider trying three last things:

Offer to mediate

You might offer to act as a mediator for one final round of negotiation. If previous negotiations have been handled clumsily, you might still be able to snatch victory from the jaws of defeat.

'Pass the hat up the chain'

Other parties in the chain might be prepared to contribute a sum of money to resolve a problem. This will often cost you less than the cost of an abortive sale. This hypothetical example shows a situation when such an offer benefits all parties:

> Property 1 sale price £50,000
> Property 2 sales price £100,000
> Property 3 sale price £150,000
> Property 4 sale price £250,000
> Property 5 sale price £500,000 (vendors moving into newly built retirement home).

A down valuation of ten per cent on Property 1 would leave the buyers £5,000 short of the funds needed to complete. To a first time buyer this would be a great deal of money. The vendors of Property 1 could not afford to concede £5,000 and the sale would fall through. However, the vendor of Property 5 could easily afford to fund the £5,000 shortfall, and it might well be in his best financial interests to do so: £5,000 represents approximately two months' loss of interest on the proceeds or one month's interest on a £500,000 mortgage.

An alternative solution might be for the vendors of Properties 3, 4 and 5 to agree to contribute £1,000, £1,000 and £3,000 respectively. This would represent approximately one month's extra mortgage for each of them.

It is surprising how often an insoluble problem can be overcome by passing the hat up the chain this way. All that is needed is someone with the knowledge and determination to negotiate it. In the absence of a better offer that someone will have to be you.

As an absolute last resort you might even consider offering to pay the disputed sum yourself either alone or in conjunction with other parties in the chain.

KNOWING WHAT TO DO IF THE CHAIN BREAKS

The suggestions given above may help you to save a sale at the eleventh hour but realistically you must accept that in many cases you will be unsuccessful.

Limiting the damage
If the chain does break, there are two last things that you might try to save the day.

Subsidising a sale lower down the chain
This is essentially a variation on passing the hat down the chain. Consider this example.

> Property 1 was sold at £50,000 to first time buyer
> Property 2 was sold at £100,000
> Property 3 was sold at £150,000
> Property 4 was sold at £250,000
> Property 5 was sold at £500,000 (the vendor was elderly and was not buying another property).

Two days before contracts were due to be exchanged the buyer of the £50,000 property withdrew for no reason. The solution which was agreed worked as follows:

> Each vendor contributed one per cent of their sale price to a communal fund thus:
>
> | | |
> |---|---|
> | Vendor 1 contributed | £500 |
> | Vendor 2 contributed | £1,000 |
> | Vendor 3 contributed | £1,500 |
> | Vendor 4 contributed | £2,500 |
> | Vendor 5 contributed | £5,000 |
> | | |
> | Total | £10,000 |

This money was used to subsidise the selling price of the £50,000 property. Thus it was put back on the market at the bargain price of £40,000. As a result it sold within hours and the chain was saved.

Sadly solutions like this rarely work because the parties let their emotions get in the way of finding a solution or because no one available has the skill, patience, motivation and tenacity to negotiate a solution that is acceptable to everybody.

Considering a part exchange
One last extreme solution to consider, if all else fails, is to offer to buy
the property that is holding up your sale as a part exchange. If you have
the funds available it is not as daft an idea as it sounds. Reconsider our
previous example. The vendor of a property selling at £500,000 and not
buying again would stand to lose a lot from a delay of three to four
months while his property is remarketed. At say six per cent per annum,
loss of interest alone comes to £2,500 per month. It might well pay a person in this position to buy a cheap property in part exchange in order to
expedite his own sale. Loss of interest on a £50,000 flat would, after all,
be only £250 per month. The cost of buying and reselling the flat would
be around £2,000. It is easy to see how the vendor could be better off.
You should at least check the sums relating to your own position on the
back of an envelope before you dismiss the idea out of hand.

Problems up the chain
All the things that could go wrong further down the chain can also go
wrong with transactions further up it. However, there is one further factor to consider if you have lost or are at risk of losing your purchase and
that is: should you still complete on your own sale? Arguments for and
against doing so are often finely balanced. Facts to consider include:

State of the market
If you are moving to a more expensive property in a buoyant market
there is a risk that prices will continue to rise while you are out of the
market. If the market is depressed you may be able to buy the next
property for less than you had anticipated.

Improved negotiating position
Without a property to sell you will be in a much stronger buying position. This may enable you to negotiate to buy your next property at a
much better price.

Cost of storage and removals
The cost of removals to and from your temporary address and/or storage
charges will be quite significant.

Non-financial factors
Moving house is extremely disruptive. You must be sure to include the
emotional cost of an extra move on both yourself and your family.

Taking all these factors into account it is probably not surprising that most vendors who lose their purchase would rather run the risk of losing their own buyer than face a double move.

CASE STUDY

Making the wrong decision

Stephen and Irene agreed a sale at exactly £100,000 on their three bed-room detached property. They were buying a four bedroom property at £150,000 and were in some hurry to find a buyer.

They left their property on the market 'just in case something went wrong with the original sale'. A week later they received a second offer for their property of £105,000. After some discussion they decided to take it. Their original buyer was furious but there was nothing that he could do about it.

Unfortunately the vendors of the house that Stephen and Irene were buying found out that their original sale had 'fallen through'. They said they could not wait any longer and sold to someone else. Stephen and Irene continued with their sale at £105,000. However, the property was down valued on survey to £100,000 and this was the price they were forced to accept.

Furthermore the only four bedroom detached house available on the estate that they wanted to move to was for sale at £160,000 and they had to agree an offer of £158,000 to get it.

Commenting on the experiences Stephen and Irene said, 'with hind-sight we should have stayed with our original buyers. We would have been £8,000 better off and we would have had the peace of mind of having behaved in a more ethical way.'

CHECKLIST

● Before you gazump your buyer make sure that you know full details about the position and time-scale of the second buyer.

● (Almost) never proceed with a purchase if your own sale falls through.

● Whatever happens remember that there will always be another property to buy.

12
Completing

PREPARING FOR EXCHANGE OF CONTRACTS

You will know that you are nearly there when your solicitor asks you to arrange an appointment to sign the contracts. Although this is certainly a good sign, you would be well advised not to relax just yet. Things can and do go wrong at the very last minute. Two problems in particular seem to occur more often than most.

Gazundering

The unscrupulous buyer knows that the later he leaves his attempt to gazunder you the more likely he is to succeed.

An attempt on the very day that exchange of contracts was due to take place is quite common. The previous advice given still applies, but the buyer knows that at this stage you are less likely to walk away from the prospect of an immediate sale and he is likely to press home his advantage quite mercilessly.

Arguments over completion dates

The longer the chain, the more difficult it will be to agree on a completion date that is acceptable to all parties. Sales have been known to break down on this point alone.

If a dispute over completion date is jeopardising your sale you should consider:

Negotiating a shorter or longer completion period

The conventional completion period is 28 days but there is no reason why it has to be. A completion period can be any length that is acceptable to both parties – a day, a week, a month, even a year; it is even possible to exchange contracts and complete simultaneously. Very short completion periods, say seven days or less, may involve your solicitor in extra work but the cost of this will be a great deal less than the cost of an abortive sale.

Agreeing to an uncoordinated completion date

If all else fails you might have to choose between moving twice or not at all. An uncoordinated completion means that you agree to vacate your property on a certain date in the knowledge that you will not get possession of your new property until, say, seven days later. The cost to you is the inconvenience of moving twice, extra removal and storage charges and probably the cost of a week's local accommodation. If the only alternative is an abortive sale, the cost could be justifiable.

PREPARING FOR COMPLETION

At long last the moment you have been waiting for arrives and your solicitor telephones to tell you that exchange of contracts has taken place. You really are nearly home and dry now and a celebration is entirely in order. Nevertheless, it is still not too late for things to go wrong.

Failure to complete

It is very, very rare for a sale not to complete at all. I have dealt with only three cases. In the first one the purchasers decided to end their marriage a few days before completion was due to take place. Neither party wanted the house and they ended up forfeiting their ten per cent deposit. In the second case the purchaser's father-in-law refused to honour a promise he had made to lend money to fund the purchase after a family row. Again the ten per cent deposit was forfeited. In the third, the vendor went insane between exchange and completion. The matter was referred to the court of protection, which took over a year to complete the sale!

ARRANGING YOUR REMOVAL

Choosing a removal firm

All removal firms are not the same. The cost of making the wrong choice could be the loss of furnishings and ornaments that have taken a lifetime to collect. The best way to choose a removal firm is by personal recommendation. Ask your friends and colleagues if they can recommend a good one. Always get more than one quotation and be sure to base the final decision on reputation as well as on price.

Deciding between removals only *v* full packing service

Most removal firms offer a variety of service levels, ranging from a full packing service where they will literally do everything, to a basic service where they provide only the lorry and a single working driver. You will need to think carefully about the service that you need to be sure that the quotations that you get from different firms are all for the same level of service.

Arranging insurance

Many otherwise reputable removal firms limit their maximum liability for loss or damage to an absurdly low amount, sometimes just a few pounds per item. There are two ways to get round this problem. The first is to arrange for the necessary additional cover through your own household insurer. The second is to find another removal firm.

Perhaps if more people did the latter the removals industry would be forced to start making proper arrangements for the protection of its customers.

Moving yourself

Moving yourself is hard work and it may not save you as much money as you think. Once you add up the cost of van hire and the hire of the chests or specialist removal cartons (without which things will get broken) you may well decide that the saving is not worth it.

If you do decide to go it alone, these tips will help things to go smoothly.

Van hire

Go to a large specialist depot. Many do an all-in removals package which includes van, carton and trolley hire. Remember that they will need to see your driving licence on the day of hiring.

Van size

If in doubt get the larger one. A larger van will allow more careful packing and reduce breakages.

Allow plenty of time

It will always take you longer than you think to move house – start early.

Anticipate making more than one journey

The contents of an average three bedroom house often do not fit into a 7.5 tonne box van (which is the largest that you can hire without an HGV licence). Allow time for a second or third journey.

Organising the utilities

Arrangements for the new house

Unless you want to move into your new home by torchlight, arrangements must be made well in advance.

- **Gas/electricity/water**. Phone the new gas, electricity and water companies. Tell them that you are taking over the supply and that you do not want the service to be discontinued. Ask for written confirmation. Be sure to read the meters as soon as you arrive at the new property.

- **Telephone**. If your new property has the same exchange code, you will have the option of keeping your old phone number. If not you will usually be given a choice between taking over your vendor's old number or having a new one. Make sure of your arrangements well in advance and ask for written confirmation.

Arrangements for the old house
Be sure to contact all the utilities to inform them that you are moving. Ask for a final account to be sent to your new address. Don't forget to read the meters before you go.

- **Mail**. The Post Office offers an excellent mail forwarding service at a very reasonable cost. It is well worth purchasing this service for at least a year in order to ensure that important post doesn't go astray. Allow at least two weeks for it to take effect.

GETTING TO THE COMPLETION DAY

Such is the perversity of the house buying process that things can go wrong even on completion day itself. Although such problems are fairly rare, it is important to keep in touch with your solicitor throughout the day. Two specific problems are worth mentioning:

Arguments over the release of keys

Your purchasers may ask if they can have the keys to your property before completion has taken place. You must never allow this, no matter what the circumstances, until your solicitor authorises it. This might be easier said than done when the purchasers are sitting on your doorstep with their removal men clocking up an overtime bill, but refuse you must. In the unlikely event of the completion not taking place the most terrible complications could arise if the buyers are already in possession.

Delay in receiving the money

The money to fund the purchase of each property in the chain will almost certainly be sent by telegraphic transfer. In this age of satellite communications you might think that money could be transferred between banks instantly. You would be wrong. The system is terribly inefficient. It often takes several hours for funds to be transferred. What is more there is a shut-off time (usually 1.00 pm) after which any funds sent will probably not arrive until the next day.

Due to the inadequacies of the system, the non-arrival of the completion monies is a fairly common problem. If you do not receive the money for your sale you will not be able to complete on your purchase, indeed completion for the whole chain could be delayed until the next day. The inconvenience, cost and legal implications of this delay can be horrendous. Every purchaser in the chain will be contractually obliged to complete by a certain time of day (usually 1.00 pm). Should they not do so they will be legally liable for any extra expenses incurred by their vendor. The result can be a lawyer's field day with everyone blaming everyone else for the delay.

Unfortunately there is not much that you can do to avoid this problem although it is worth phoning your solicitor at around 12.00 midday to check that everything is OK. If there is a problem you will have at least an hour to solve it.

ARRIVING AT YOUR NEW HOUSE

Congratulations. You have done it – but before you completely relax it is worth doing three last things:

1. **Test the services**. Check immediately that you have gas, electricity, water and a telephone. If any of these services have been disconnected you will need to get onto the suppliers immediately.

2. **Read the meters**. It is all too easy to get caught for the previous owner's bill. Check the meters and make a careful note of the readings as soon as you move in.

3. **Check the fixtures and fittings list**. Check to make sure that all fixtures and fittings that should have been left have been. If something major has been taken in defiance of the contracted agreement you can threaten to sue for its return.

CASE STUDY

Biting the bullet

Just an hour before contracts were due to be exchanged Bernard received a phone call from his agent to say that the buyer had reduced her offer from £95,000 to £90,000 and said take it or leave it.

Bernard was beside himself with worry – he was due to start a new job 500 miles away in four weeks' time and could not afford the delay. The rest of the day was a battle of nerves but the sale did eventually exchange at £92,500.

Commenting on his experience Bernard said, 'I feel that I was cheated out of £2,500 but it would have cost me a lot more to back out of the sale and my buyer knew this so I just had to bite the bullet.'

CHECKLIST

● Choose your removal firm on service and reputation, not just on price.

● Check the insurance position if your furniture is lost in transit.

● Allow plenty of time: moving always takes longer than you think.

● Double-check arrangements for the telephone, post and utilities.

● Don't expect to get the keys until the money has been paid. Think about what you will do if the money does not arrive for any reason.

● Check the gas, electricity and water as soon as you arrive at the new property.

● Read the meters on arrival.

● Check that all fixtures and fittings that should have been left have been.

THE LAST WORD

Moving house will never be easy, but I hope that this book has helped you to avoid some of the common pitfalls. All that remains now is to enjoy your new home.

And this book. Well, this book might serve one last useful purpose. I would suggest that you put it on a bookshelf in a prominent position so that if, at any time in the future, you find yourself thinking, 'wouldn't it be nice to have an extra bedroom?' you can look at the cover and ask yourself – is it really worth it?

13
Forthcoming Legislation

Throughout this book I have complained bitterly about the inefficiency of the English house buying process. Now at last it seems that this is about to change.

At the beginning of 1998, the Government embarked upon a far-reaching review of the house buying process. In December 1998 it published a consultation document entitled *The Key to Easier House Buying and Selling*. This consultation paper has recommended that the whole process should be changed fundamentally.

The nub of the Government's proposal is that sellers should, in future, be required to prepare a 'seller's pack' before they put their property onto the market. This information pack would be available to all prospective purchasers from the very outset. The proposal is that the pack should include:

- copy title deeds (office copy entries) or copies of unregistered documents of title

- a property information form containing the seller's replies to standard pre-contract enquiries

- replies to standard search and other enquiries made of the local authority

- copies of consents relating to planning and listed building consents and building regulations

- for new properties, copies of warranties and guarantees

- any available guarantees for works carried out (*eg* damp proofing, timber preservation, cavity wall insulation *etc*)

- a survey report on the condition of the property, including requirements for urgent or significant repairs or matters requiring further investigation

● a draft contract.

For leasehold properties the pack should also include copies of:

● the lease

● the most recent service charge accounts and receipts

● the insurance policy covering the building and receipts for premiums

● current regulations made by the landlord or management company

● memorandum and articles of the landlord or management company.

The availability of this information from the outset would be of benefit to both buyers and sellers. The main benefits are:

● average transaction times would be reduced

● there would be less need for subsequent renegotiation of the price or other terms of the sale

● there would be less chance of the sale falling through

● there would be less chance of the buyer and seller incurring abortive legal fees and survey fees.

However, these benefits would come at a price. The cost of producing this information pack is likely to be between £400 and £700 for an averaged sized property (at least a hundred pounds more than the combined cost of legal fees and survey fees under the current system). More significantly, the vendor would, in future, need to find this money before putting their property onto the market rather than paying the fees out of the proceeds of the sale.

OVERCOMING THE DIFFICULTIES

Despite the additional costs that would be imposed on vendors, reaction to the consultation document has been generally positive and it seems likely that the Government will implement most of its recommendations. However, before such major changes to the process can be introduced, the Government will have to overcome some substantial difficulties. These include the following.

Cost resistance

Sellers will undoubtedly be reluctant to pay for the cost of producing a seller's information pack before they put their property onto the market. The system will not work unless all vendors comply. The only way to achieve this will be to pass legislation that makes it a criminal or civil offence to offer a property for sale without the necessary documentation. It will take at least two years to draft the necessary legislation and find parliamentary time to pass it.

Impartiality of survey

Buyers may be reluctant to rely upon a survey report that has been commissioned by the vendor. This problem is compounded by the fact that at the moment, a surveyor owes a duty of care only to the person who commissioned the survey report. Thus if the vendor commissions a survey and the buyer relies upon it, the buyer cannot sue the surveyor in the event that he fails to point out a defect.

This will have to change. Before vendor surveys are made compulsory, buyers will have to be given a legal right of redress against the surveyor in the event that a defect is missed. This could be achieved through a change in working practices without the need for legislation.

Duplication of survey reports

Much of the benefit of the pre-market survey will be lost if mortgage lenders continue to require their own surveyor to conduct a post-offer mortgage valuation. It is difficult to see how the property could be valued by the vendor's surveyor. Apart from the conflict of interest, the valuation would go out of date very quickly if the property remained on the market for any length of time. Nevertheless, a system that requires two surveyors to visit the same property is clearly duplicitous and undesirable.

I believe that this problem will be resolved through commercial pressures. The process will start when a mortgage lender tries to gain a commercial advantage by dropping their requirement for a mortgage valuation in cases where the loan required does not exceed, say, 70 per cent of the purchase price. Another lender might then say that they will drop the requirement for a mortgage valuation if the loan required does not exceed 80 per cent of the purchase price. Eventually, free market competition will lead to lenders dropping the requirement for a second survey in most cases. Instead, lenders will rely for their security on:

● The vendor's own survey report (which now gives both the lender and the borrower a legal right of redress if a defect is missed).

● The creditworthiness of the borrower.

● Possibly, an on-line check with the Land Registry to determine the selling price of similar properties in the area (this is not possible at the moment. However, it seems likely that the Land Registry will soon start to release the actual selling prices achieved for all properties and make this information available on-line).

If the buyer's creditworthiness is in doubt, if the vendor's survey shows that there are serious defects with the property or if the Land Registry search shows that the price agreed is out of line with prices paid for similar properties in the area, the mortgage lender may require its own survey. However, in most cases, I believe that this requirement will be dropped.

Resistance by solicitors
The Government's proposals will not cause extra work for conveyancing solicitors. However, the reduction in the average transaction times will put conveyancing solicitors under pressure to work much more quickly. A second consequence is that vendors will have to instruct their solicitor to prepare an information pack before they put their property onto the market.

I believe that the consequence of this will be an increase in the number of large specialised conveyancing firms. These firms will conduct business in a very different way from the traditional high street solicitor. This has already begun to happen. Some firms, for example, Hambro Conveyancing already offer an express conveyancing service which is open on Saturdays and Sundays and late into the evening. I believe that many more such firms will appear.

Poor co-operation between the professions
Solicitors, surveyors and estate agents do not get on with each other particularly well. This will have to change. The new house buying process will require far greater co-operation between the professionals. My prediction is that this is likely to lead to the creation of mixed practices

where solicitors, estate agents and surveyors work under one roof to offer a one-stop service.

Inability of vendors to pay up-front costs

Some vendors, particularly those who are selling because of financial difficulties, may not be able to afford to pay for a seller's pack before they put their property onto the market. This is another problem which will probably be resolved by commercial pressures.

It seems likely that in order to gain a commercial advantage some firms of solicitors and estate agents may pay the cost of producing the vendor pack themselves and recoup it by charging a higher fee when the transaction completes.

Delays with Land Registry searches

The Land Registry is already quite efficient and office copy entries are usually supplied within ten working days. This time scale could be reduced further once this information is available on-line.

Delays can arise, however, when a property is unregistered. A consequence of these changes could be pressure for the compulsory registration of all remaining unregistered properties.

Delays with local authority searches

Many sales are held up by delays in obtaining local searches. Some local authorities are extremely inefficient. The worst take several weeks to respond to a search request. This will have to change. The solution is to impose statutory time limits for responding to a search request with sanctions available to use against local authorities that do not comply. If persuasion doesn't work, this may require legislation.

Delays caused by the buyer's mortgage application

Some mortgage lenders take more than a month to deal with a mortgage application. This could undermine all attempts to speed up the process. The solution is to encourage buyers to apply for a mortgage in principle before they start looking for a property. This would mean that employment and financial references could be taken up in advance. Once a buyer finds a property, a mortgage offer could be made within a few days.

This change is also likely to be achieved by commercial pressures. My prediction is that in future, prospective buyers will not be taken seriously unless they have arranged a mortgage in principle.

Difficulty in building chains

A reduction in average transaction times may make it more difficult to co-ordinate transactions and build chains. The solution to this problem is likely to come in the form of more flexible and more widely available bridging finance. At the moment, the interest on most bridging loans must be paid in full on a monthly basis. This makes a bridging loan prohibitively expensive for most people. In future it may be possible to add the cost of bridging finance onto the main mortgage loan and pay it off over the full term of the mortgage. This would make bridging finance far more affordable.

IMPLEMENTING THE CHANGES

Some of these changes will require legislation. The constraint here will be the availability of parliamentary time. Others will require only a change in working practices or the design of new products and services. However, solicitors, surveyors and estate agents will need time to design and develop new products and train their staff to deliver them. Taking this into account I would predict it will be at least two years, *ie* early in the year 2001, before all these changes can be implemented.

ANTICIPATING THE CHANGES

However, some changes will be bought in sooner and you may be able to gain an advantage by responding to them quickly. For example, if you are selling a property there is no reason why you should not compile a partial seller's pack for your property now. This would mean that you would have to instruct your solicitor a little sooner but you would not incur any additional costs. The benefit is that by making more information available, you may persuade a prospective purchaser to buy your property in preference to another.

At the present time this seller's information pack could include:

● copies of title documents

● replies to standard preliminary enquiries made on behalf of buyers

● copies of any planning, listed building and building regulation consents and approvals

● for new properties, copies of warranties and guarantees

● any guarantees for work carried out on the property

● a draft contract.

If your property is leasehold you might also include a copy of:

- the lease

- recent accounts and receipts for service charges

- building insurance policy and receipts for premiums

- regulations made by the landlord or management company

- the landlord or management company's memorandum and articles.

It may also be worth applying for local searches at the time that you put the property onto the market. The drawback is that if the property is not sold quickly, the searches may get out of date which would mean that the search fee would have been wasted.

Some estate agents and surveyors may start to offer vendor surveys on a voluntary basis in advance of legislation. However, under the present system I can see limited benefit in paying for one.

So long as mortgage lenders require their own surveyor to do a valuation, you will not save any time by commissioning your own survey and so long as the surveyor's liability is restricted to the person who commissions the report, your buyer will be reluctant to rely upon any report that you commission.

If you are also buying a property there may be considerable advantage in applying for a mortgage in principle. This will prove that you are creditworthy and could save quite a bit of time once you find a property.

There is no doubt that such a fundamental change to the house buying process will cause considerable disruption and confusion. Nevertheless, I believe that the revised process will be quicker and less stressful for all concerned and a certain amount of disruption in the short term is a price that is well worth paying to achieve this.

As soon as the result of the consultation process is known, we will bring out a revised edition of this book.

Glossary

AGENTS' TERMS

Applicant. A potential purchaser enquiring for a property to buy.

Company move. A term used to describe a move with financial assistance from employers.

Corporate estate agents. A term used to describe the firms of estate agents who are owned by the financial institutions.

Dependent sale. A term used to describe a sale to a purchaser who has to sell their property before being in a financial position to proceed.

Disinstruction. A vendor advises they no longer wish their property to be offered for sale.

Financial services. An umbrella term used to describe mortgage arrangements and insurance policies which are offered to clients and customers.

Financial consultant. Somebody who is qualified under the financial services act to give financial advice.

Gazumping. A term used when a vendor accepts a higher offer after agreeing a sale with a purchaser subject to contract.

Gazundering. A term that is used when a purchaser reduces the offer that they have made for a property at the very last moment.

Independent estate agents. A term used to describe the estate agency firms which are still owned by private individuals or companies and which are not linked to a financial institution.

Joint sole agency. A term used to describe an agency where two or more agents agree to share the commission regardless of which of them achieves the sale.

Lettings. A term used to describe the renting rather than selling of property.

Listing. A term used to describe property that has been taken onto the market for sale.

Mortgage valuation. A valuation for the lender of mortgage finance.

Multi-agency. A term used to describe the situation where two or more

135

agents are instructed to sell a property on terms where the first agent to achieve a sale will earn the entire commission.

No chain. A sale where the vendor and purchaser are not buying or selling other properties.

Personal interest. An estate agent is not allowed to purchase a property that his/her employer is selling without declaring a personal interest to the vendors. Agents must also declare a personal interest when they are selling a property which they own through the firm that employs them.

PMA. An abbreviation for the Property Misdescriptions Act 1991.

Relocation. A term used to describe moving to a different part of the country with financial assistance from their employer.

Repossession. A property that has been repossessed by the mortgagees due to the non-payment of the mortgage.

Retention. A sum of money which is held back by a mortgage lender until certain specified works have been completed to a required standard.

Sole agency. The term used to describe an agent who is appointed as the only agent who will be offering a property for sale during a given period.

Survey. A visit to a property by a surveyor who will compile a report on the structural conditions and/or value of a property.

Take-on. A property that has been taken onto the market for sale.

Touting. A direct approach to the vendors of properties which are being offered for sale by another estate agent. NB: The NAEA have specific rules governing this.

Under offer. An alternative term for a property that is sold subject to contract.

Vacant possession. A property which will be vacant on completion day.

Valuation. When a potential vendor invites the agent to value their house with a view to putting the property on the market.

Vendor. The person who is selling a property.

LEGAL TERMS

Contract. A legal document setting out the terms under which a sale will take place.

Covenant. A restriction on the use of a freehold property (*eg* it must be used for residential purposes only).

Deeds. The legal documents that prove ownership of a property.

Exchange of contracts. The point at which the sale usually becomes binding.

Flying freehold. A freehold property, all or part of which is supported by another adjoining property as opposed to being connected to the ground.

Freehold. A property which is owned in perpetuity.

Leasehold. A property that the owner will only be able to use for certain term. Many leases are originally granted for 99 years. At the end of this time ownership of the property will revert to the freeholder.

Legal executive. Somebody who works for a legal firm undertaking legal work, but is not a qualified solicitor.

Legal completion. The day upon which money is paid and the purchaser usually has the right to occupy the property.

Licensed conveyancer. Somebody other than a solicitor who is licensed to undertake conveyancing work.

Memorandum of sale. A summary of the main terms and conditions for a sale which is sent out to the vendor, purchaser and both solicitors when a sale is first agreed.

Mortgage offer. A binding promise by a mortgage lender to lend money to a purchaser of a property usually with conditions.

Mortgage indemnity. An insurance policy which protects a lender from incurring financial loss in the event that a property is sold for less than the mortgage secured on it.

Mortgage retention. When the property requires work the mortgage lender will occasionally retain a portion of the mortgage funds until such time as that work has been completed to their satisfaction.

Policy. An insurance policy which covers a mortgage lender against losses that might be incurred in the event that a property is sold for a lower price than the amount of the outstanding mortgage.

Outline planning. When the local authority has given approval for an outline scheme which is then followed by detailed proposals.

Planning permission. Permission granted by the local council for development or a change of use to a property.

Probate sale. A term used to describe the sale of a property where the owner is deceased.

Repayment mortgage. A conventional type of mortgage where money is borrowed and repaid with interest over the full term.

Search. An enquiry that is made of the local authority to check that nothing adverse is likely to happen in the immediate vicinity (such as a new road scheme).

Sold subject to contract. An offer has been accepted but exchange of contracts have not taken place.

Solicitor. Somebody who is qualified by the Law Society to give legal advice.

PROPERTY TERMS

Air bricks. Bricks with ventilation holes in them to allow air to circulate beneath the floors of a building.

Annexe. A self-contained portion of a large house. An annexe is often used to house an elderly relative.

Bay fronted. A property where the windows protrude from the front wall of the property.

Block insurance. A type of building insurance policy that covers all the flats in a building.

Box bay. A bay window built in an oblong shape with two 90 degree corners.

Bungalow. A single storey dwelling.

Canopy porch. A porch comprising of a roof only with open sides.

Capped chimney. A chimney which has been sealed at the top to prevent the entry of birds and or dampness.

Casement window. Type of window which is hinged at the top, side or bottom.

Cavity walls. A form of construction whereby two brick walls are built with a small space between them. This form of construction provides much better stability and weather protection.

Chalet bungalow. A bungalow with some first floor rooms built under the slope of the roof.

Cylinder lock. A lock which can be opened from the inside without a key (*eg* a Yale lock).

Detached. A house which is not joined to any other building on any side.

Dormer window. A type of window which protrudes from a pitched roof, allowing the glass to be held in a vertical position.

Double bay. A property with two bay windows.

Double garage. A garage where two cars can be parked side by side.

Double glazing. Two layers of glass held in place by a single frame usually with the purpose of reducing heat loss through the windows.

En-suite bathroom. A bathroom for the sole use of a bedroom and with a connecting door.

Ex-Council. A house that was originally built for rent by the local authority.

Gas radiator central heating. A gas boiler which heats a property using panel radiators through which flows hot water.

Fitted wardrobes. A wardrobe which is built into a part of the property.

Flat roof. A horizontal roof often covered in felt, which requires regular renewal.

Flat. A self-contained portion of a building with its own kitchen and bathroom facilities.

Gable. The triangular shaped vertical portion of wall at the end of the roof.

Gas warm air. A type of heating system where a gas boiler is used to heat air, which is circulated through ducts to each room of the property with the assistance of an electrical fan.

Ground rent. An annual rental made to the freeholder under the terms of a long lease.

Hard standing. A cement or tarmac area designed for the parking of a motor vehicle.

House insurance. Another term for building insurance which covers the owner of the property.

Integral garage. A garage which is built within the walls of the main property and could have access to the property via an integral door.

Leaded light. The small panes of glass often seen in cottage windows.

Link detached. A detached house with an attached garage which is attached to another adjoining building.

Loft conversion. A term used to describe a room or rooms which have been formed in what was originally the roof space.

Maisonette. A flat with its own front door which has access direct to the outside, as opposed to via a communal hallway, or a two or more storey flat.

Mortice lock. A lock which cannot be opened from either side without a key and is set within the body of the door.

Oil fired central heating. Central heating which is powered by an oil burning boiler.

Open plan. A house with no internal walls to separate the living room, the dining room and the kitchen.

Open fireplace. A fireplace which is designed for use with a coal or log fire.

Pitched roof. The traditional style of roof pitched at an angle and usually covered in slate or tiles.

Purlin. One of the timbers supporting a pitched roof. A purlin is the timber that supports the rafters to stop sagging.

Quarter back. A group of houses built in a square with two outside walls and two walls shared with the adjoining properties.

Reception room. An old-fashioned term to describe the main living rooms.

Render. A sand and cement coating applied to the external wall of a property and often painted or textured.

Roof trusses. The larger triangulated structures usually built of timber which support the main weight of the roof.

RSJ. A steel beam which supports the weight of a structure over an opening.

Sash windows. The type of window which slides vertically up and downwards.

Secondary glazing. Two layers of glass held in place by two separate frames with the purpose of reducing either heat loss or improving sound insulation on a window.

Shared driveway. A driveway which is shared with one or more other properties.

Single storey extension. A single storey extension built onto a property.

Single skin extension. An extension with a wall constructed of a single layer of brick. Such extensions are usually not suitable for permanent habitation.

Skylight windows. A window which is at the same angle as the pitched roof itself.

Split level. A house where each storey is built on more than one level, such houses are usually built on a hill side.

Stone cladding. A thin layer of stone or imitation stone which is attached to the external wall of a property.

Storage heater. A type of electric heating which heats up by using cheap electricity available at night and discharges this heat throughout the day.

Stud wall. An internal wall made from a wooden frame rather than brick.

Studio. A type of small flat comprising of one room which is used for living, sleeping and cooking, together with a separate bathroom.

Tandem garage. A double length garage where two vehicles are parked one behind the other.

Terraced house. A house that is joined to the adjoining buildings on both sides.

Thatched roof. A roof which is covered with straw or reeds rather than tiles.

Tile hung. Tiles hung on a vertical wall either for decorative purposes or to keep out dampness.

Timber frame construction. A form of construction where the building is based around a timber frame taking the load.

Timber treatment. Any treatment to the timber in a property, *eg* woodworm, dry rot or wet rot.

Town house. A three or four storey house with integral garage occupying the ground floor. Usually found in town centre locations where living space and parking space is at a premium and usually in a terrace.

Traditional construction. The traditional form of building where the external walls of the property are of masonry construction and load bearing.

UPVC. An abbreviation for a particular type of plastic window frame.

Wall tie. A metal tie that connects the inner and outer sections of a cavity wall in order to improve the structural stability.

TECHNICAL TERMS

Contents insurance. An insurance policy that protects a householder in the event of their furniture or other contents being lost, damaged or stolen.

Detailed planning permission. The permission for development according to detailed planning specifications.

Dot screen photo. A special type of photograph designed for clear reproduction on a photocopier.

Dry rot. A type of fungus which can cause serious damage to a building.

Endowment. A type of combined savings and life assurance policy often sold as a vehicle to repay a mortgage at a future date with interest only being paid during the term.

Fixtures and fittings. A collective term that is applied to any removable fixtures or fittings which may or may not be included in the sale price.

Penetrating damp. Dampness that is penetrating through the walls, usually as a result of a defect such as a crack or perhaps a leaking drainpipe.

Re-pointing. The restoration of the mortar between the bricks on an external wall.

Rising damp. Dampness which is transmitted up from the ground due to a failure or absence of a dampcourse.

Septic tank. A method of disposing of sewage when a property is not connected to a main sewer.

Structural survey. A comprehensive survey which reports in detail on the condition of a property.

Structural engineer's report. A specialist report on a property where there is evidence of structural movement or a potential risk.

Subsidence. Structural damage caused to a property due to its sinking into the ground.

Wet rot. Wood that has rotted because of it being saturated by damp.

Useful Addresses

British Association of Removers, 279 Grays Inn Road, London WC2 8SY. Tel: (0171) 837 3088.

The Incorporated Society of Valuers and Auctioneers, 3 Cadogan Gate, London SW1X 0AS. Tel: (0171) 235 2282.

The Law Society, 113 Chancery Lane, London WC2A 1EL. Tel: (0171) 242 1222.

The Law Society of Scotland, PO Box 75, 26 Drumsheugh Gardens, Edinburgh EH3 7YR. Tel: (0131) 226 7411.

National Association of Conveyancers, 2/4 Chichester Rents, Chancery Lane, London WC2A 1EG. Tel: (0171) 405 8582.

The National Association of Estate Agents, Arbon House, 21 Jury Street, Warwick CV34 4EH. Tel: (01926) 496800.

The Royal Institution of Chartered Surveyors, 12 Great George Street, Parliament Square, London SW1P 3AD. Tel: (0171) 222 7000.

Appendix 1
Sample Sole Agency Agreement

PALMER SNELL.
Standard Terms and Conditions

INTRODUCTION

This document sets out the terms and conditions under which Palmer Snell will act for you in the sale of your property.

If you wish to instruct us, our Instruction Agreement is to be found opposite. When completed, it should be signed both by you (or a person acting on your behalf) as "Seller" and by a representative of Palmer Snell.

Additional specific items may be set out in greater detail in an accompanying letter which the Seller is requested to sign and return as acceptance of such items.

CHOOSING THE RIGHT AGENT

This is without doubt the most important decision that you will need to make.

At Palmer Snell we believe that there is only one choice. The majority of our instructions come from satisfied clients who have used our services previously and through recommendations.

Having successfully sold properties since 1811, there is hardly a problem that we have not encountered and solved. This is due to our experienced and fully trained residential sales teams located in every office throughout the area. Our high profile offices, backed by extensive local and regional advertising, sets us apart from the rest.

YOU CAN INSTRUCT US ON ANY OF THE FOLLOWING TERMS:-

1. SOLE AGENCY

Commission of _____ % of the Agreed sale price plus VAT.

You will be liable to pay remuneration to us, in addition to any other costs or charges agreed, if at any time unconditional contracts for the sale of the property are exchanged-

with a purchaser introduced by us during the periods of our sole agency or with whom we had negotiations about the property during that period; or with a purchaser introduced by another agent during that period.

2. MULTIPLE AGENCY

Commission of _____ % of the agreed sale price plus VAT.

You will be liable to pay remuneration to us, in addition to any other costs or charges agreed, if at any time unconditional contracts for the sale of the property are exchanged with a purchaser introduced by us (whether directly or indirectly).

3. JOINT SOLE AGENCY

Commission of _____ % of the agreed sale price plus VAT.

You will be liable to pay remuneration to us, in addition to any other costs or charges agreed, if at any time unconditional contracts for the sale of the property are exchanged-

with a purchaser introduced by either of the Joint Sole Agents during the period of our sole agency or with whom we had negotiations about the property during that period;

The commission will be shared between the instructed Joint Sole Agents at their discretion.

Please note that we are obliged to define 'Sole Agency' in accordance with the Estate Agents Act 1979 and supplemental Regulations ('The Act')

References to an introduction by Palmer Snell will include both direct and indirect introductions.

SUB-AGENCY

If we consider that it may be of assistance in effecting a sale (and providing that you have expressed no prior objection) we may appoint a sub-agent(s), and references to results being achieved through our agency will include the case where results have been achieved in whole or in part through any such sub-agent.

FEES

The commission will become due for payment upon exchange of contracts and payable upon completion. VAT at the rate in force at exchange of contracts will be payable on the commission.

The Seller confirms that instruction will be given to a Solicitor, Conveyancer or other legal representative, to pay the commission on the date of completion.

Interest will be charged on any outstanding sum at 3% over the National Westminster Bank PLC base rate and will run from the date of completion, should the account not be paid within 7 days.

PART EXCHANGE

In the event of Palmer Snell introducing an applicant who proceeds with a part exchange deal the normal commission will be payable. The commission will be calculated on the aggregate sum of the cash exchange (if any) plus the value of the purchasers part exchanged property.

EXPENSES

Any additional marketing costs (such as advertising, brochures photography) and other expenses will be agreed in writing with you and (if applicable) become payable upon invoicing.

Palmer Snell reserve the right to retain or share the benefit of any marketing discounts and commissions.

OTHER SERVICES

Palmer Snell offers a wide variety of related services, such as Valuations (Residential, Business and Commercial), Property Auctions, New Homes Sales, Residential Letting and Management, Survey and Professional Services, Commercial Sales and Others. Full details are available upon request.

MORTGAGE ADVICE

We will offer all prospective purchasers, without obligation, guidance with their proposed purchase including comprehensive mortgage advice. This advice is also available to sellers prior to marketing their property or alternatively at the time an offer is received from a prospective purchaser.

With nearly 100 Building Societies as well as the High Street Banks all claiming to offer attractive mortgage terms understanding the differences can be daunting. Palmer Snell has solved this problem with a personalised computerised search facility for which no charge is made. Further information available from your local office.

Palmer Snell is an introducer to London and Manchester (Agency Financial Services) Limited which is a Representative only of the London and Manchester Marketing Group. Members of which are regulated by the Personal Investment Authority and IMRO.

"FOR SALE" BOARDS

"For Sale" boards are an extremely important marketing tool. They advertise that the property is FOR SALE twenty-four hours a day, seven days a week; we cannot recommend their use strongly enough.

Under current legislation only one "For Sale" board is permitted outside each property. Contravention of this may result in Palmer Snell and the Seller liable to prosecution by the Local Authority. If it is agreed that Palmer Snell should have permission to erect a "For Sale" board and if another agent, with or without your consent, should erect another "For Sale" sign please advise us immediately.

PERSONAL INTEREST

Under the Act, we must disclose to you in writing if Palmer Snell or any connected person has a personal interest in your property or is seeking to acquire a beneficial interest in the property, or in the proceeds of a sale of any such interest.

TERMINATION OF AGREEMENT

If there is a minimum period stated in the Instruction Agreement. Cancellation of the Agreement may be only on the expiry of 14 days written notice given by either party at the end of this minimum period.

Cancellation of any Agreement where a minimum period is not stated may be made on the expiry of 14 days written notice by either party.

PROPERTY MISDESCRIPTIONS ACT 1991

We are obliged to present the details, photographs and advertising, in compliance with the above Act. This means that no false or misleading statements may be made and we would seek your understanding and co-operation in achieving this objective.

Reproduced by kind permission of Palmer Snell.

INSTRUCTION AGREEMENT

DATE:...   Ref. No. [   ]

CONTACT: ....

CODE.....................................:OFFICE: ....

PROPERTY ADDRESS ....

....

SELLER(S)...

SELLER(S) ADDRESS ....

....

TEL HOME..TEL WORK...........................

SOLICITOR ....CONTACT ....

ADDRESS ....TEL.............

PRICE to be quoted £ ....FREEHOLD/LEASEHOLD*/LENGTH OF LEASE...................

SERVICE CHARGE & GROUND RENT ....HOW ARE THESE CALCULATED ....

ARE THERE ANY SHARED/COMMUNAL AREAS ....

FIXTURES & FITTINGS .... Negotiable/Included*

CONSTRUCTION OF THE PROPERTY ....

ARE THERE ANY GUARANTEES...

ARE YOU AWARE OF ANY OF THE FOLLOWING:-

Restrictive covenants   Yes/No* details ....

Dispute with neighbours etc.   Yes/No* details ....

Highway or planning proposals   Yes/No* details ....

Rights of way, that affect the property Yes/No* details ....

Alterations to the property   Yes/No* details ....

If yes was planning consent & building requirements obtained Yes/No details...........................

SERVICES CONNECTED   Mains Gas Yes/No   Propane Gas Yes/No   Mains Water Yes/No

                       Mains Elec Yes/No   Drainage Mains/Private   if private Cesspit/Septic Tank

POSSESSION (When are you likely to be able to complete)..

PRESENT MORTGAGE ARRANGEMENTS:-...

VALUATION ADVICE ....

COMMISSION: It is agreed that PALMER SNELL are appointed as SOLE/MULTIPLE AGENTS* for a period of

not less than   weeks from today's date at a commission rate of   % of the agreed selling price plus VAT.

OTHER COMMISSION ARRANGEMENTS:-...

ADDITIONAL EXPENSES (where applicable)...

OTHER AGENTS INSTRUCTED:-...

SELLERS PURCHASE ARRANGEMENTS ....

PROPERTY DETAILS						APPEARANCE	AGE	
HOUSE	HO	TERRACED	BEDS	No of	SHARED GARDEN	VERY GOOD	PERIOD	
BUNGALOW	BU	END-TERR	BATH'S	No of	NO GARDEN	GOOD	OLD	
CHALET	CH	SEMI-DET			SMALL GARDEN	AVERAGE	MODERN	
FLAT	FL	DET-LINK	RECEP	No of	MEDIUM GARDEN	POOR	NON-ESTATE	
GROUND FLOOR FLAT	GF	DETACHED	GARAGES	No of	LARGE GARDEN	STR DEFECT	SMALL DEV.	
COTTAGE	CO		PARK SPACE No.		LAND ACREAGE	RENOVATION	ESTATE	
MAISONETTE	MA	OUTBUILDINGS						
BUILDING PLOT	BL	ANNEXE/FLAT						
WARDEN FLAT	WA							
BARN CONVERSIONS	BN		AREA CODE OF PROPERTY				TOWN/RURAL	

CONNECTED PERSON*....................................... FOR SALE BOARD YES/NO*.......................

VIEWING   By Appt. ☐   Key Un Accompanied ☐   Key Accompany ☐

ARRANGEMENTS ....

I/We* confirm that I/we* have read and agree to Palmer Snell's Standard Terms and Conditions and the information given
above is complete and correct. I/We* acknowledge receipt of the Standard Terms and Conditions and of a duplicate of
this Instruction Agreement. I/We* warrant that, in the event of the property being held in co-ownership, I/We* have
authority to sign this Agreement.

....

Seller   *Delete where necessary   on behalf of Palmer Snell

Reproduced by kind permission of Palmer Snell.

Appendix 2
Black Horse Agencies
Home Buyers' Report
February 1998

Average time taken to sell a property

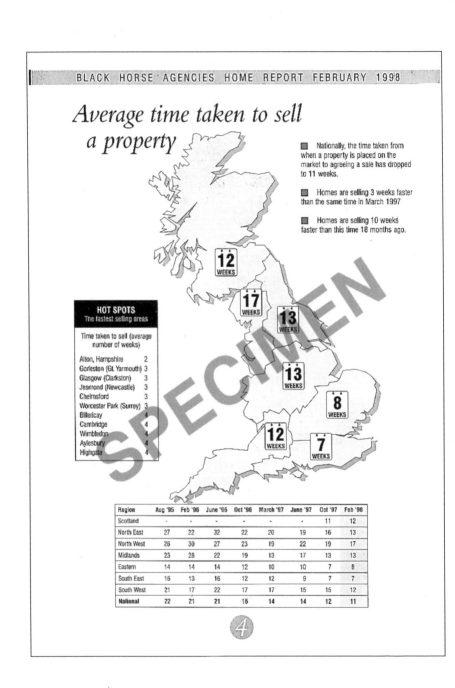

■ Nationally, the time taken from when a property is placed on the market to agreeing a sale has dropped to 11 weeks.

■ Homes are selling 3 weeks faster than the same time in March 1997

■ Homes are selling 10 weeks faster than this time 18 months ago.

12 WEEKS

17 WEEKS

13 WEEKS

13 WEEKS

8 WEEKS

12 WEEKS

7 WEEKS

HOT SPOTS
The fastest selling areas

Time taken to sell (average number of weeks)

Alton, Hampshire	2
Gorleston (Gt. Yarmouth)	3
Glasgow (Clarkston)	3
Jesmond (Newcastle)	3
Chelmsford	3
Worcester Park (Surrey)	3
Billericay	4
Cambridge	4
Wimbledon	4
Aylesbury	4
Highgate	4

Region	Aug '95	Feb '96	June '96	Oct '96	March '97	June '97	Oct '97	Feb '98
Scotland	-	-	-	-	-	-	11	12
North East	27	22	32	22	20	19	16	13
North West	28	30	27	23	19	22	19	17
Midlands	23	28	22	19	13	17	13	13
Eastern	14	14	14	12	10	10	7	8
South East	16	13	16	12	12	9	7	7
South West	21	17	22	17	17	15	15	12
National	22	21	21	16	14	14	12	11

④

Reproduced by kind permission of Black Horse Agencies.

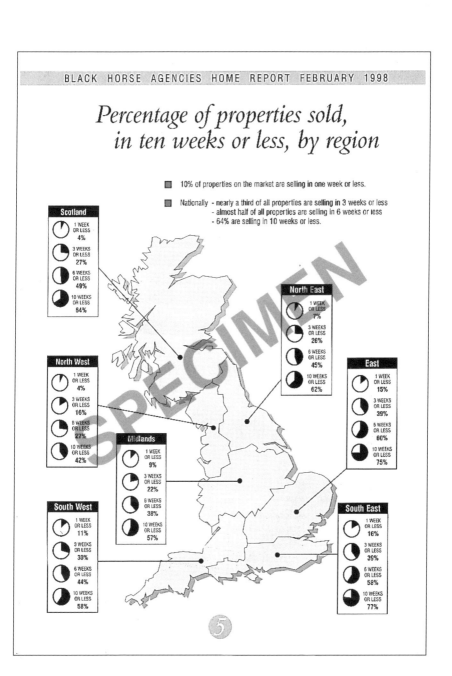

BLACK HORSE AGENCIES HOME REPORT FEBRUARY 1998

Percentage of properties sold, in ten weeks or less, by region

■ 10% of properties on the market are selling in one week or less.

■ Nationally - nearly a third of all properties are selling in 3 weeks or less
- almost half of all properties are selling in 6 weeks or less
- 64% are selling in 10 weeks or less.

Scotland
- 1 WEEK OR LESS 4%
- 3 WEEKS OR LESS 27%
- 6 WEEKS OR LESS 49%
- 10 WEEKS OR LESS 64%

North East
- 1 WEEK OR LESS 7%
- 3 WEEKS OR LESS 26%
- 6 WEEKS OR LESS 45%
- 10 WEEKS OR LESS 62%

North West
- 1 WEEK OR LESS 4%
- 3 WEEKS OR LESS 16%
- 6 WEEKS OR LESS 27%
- 10 WEEKS OR LESS 42%

East
- 1 WEEK OR LESS 15%
- 3 WEEKS OR LESS 39%
- 6 WEEKS OR LESS 60%
- 10 WEEKS OR LESS 75%

Midlands
- 1 WEEK OR LESS 9%
- 3 WEEKS OR LESS 22%
- 6 WEEKS OR LESS 38%
- 10 WEEKS OR LESS 57%

South West
- 1 WEEK OR LESS 11%
- 3 WEEKS OR LESS 30%
- 6 WEEKS OR LESS 44%
- 10 WEEKS OR LESS 58%

South East
- 1 WEEK OR LESS 16%
- 3 WEEKS OR LESS 39%
- 6 WEEKS OR LESS 58%
- 10 WEEKS OR LESS 77%

Reproduced by kind permission of Black Horse Agencies.

151

Appendix 3
Sample Building Society
Report and Valuation

Report and Valuation for Mortgage

WOOLWICH
— BUILDING SOCIETY —

Property		Age of proposed security
		Early 1900s

Applicant	Occupation: Owner/Tenant/Vacant*	Date
	Owner	

Tenure: Freehold/Leasehold/Feudal*	Years unexpired	Home branch
Leasehold	82 years	

Ground rent	Fixed/Escalating*	Introducing branch
£30 pa		

Description:

TYPE & AGE: A self-contained first and second floor maisonette conversion in an early 1900's inner-terraced house on ground and upper floors

CONSTRUCTION: Brick construction, front elevation fully colour-washed, under pitched concrete tiled roof. Timber inter-floor.

ACCOMMODATION:
GROUND FLOOR: Stairs to:-
FIRST FLOOR: Hall, living room, kitchen/breakfast room, bathroom/wc.
SECOND FLOOR: Landing, 2 attic double bedrooms.
OUTSIDE: There is no outside space.
SERVICES: All mains services including gas central heating.
ROADS: Made up, paved and adopted

Superficial gross floor area
76 sq.m.

Condition, repairs required & general comment:
The property provides spacious two double bedroom accommodation with the benefit of a large living room with coal effect gas fire and a kitchen/breakfast room. All windows except to the living room have been replaced with UPVC double-glazed units. The property has generally been well maintained with the following exceptions:-

1. The clap boarding to the front dormer is rotting and requires repair/renewal and redecoration.

2. There is slight vertical cracking over the entrance porch lintel and vertically to either side of the two storey front bay. These appear to be longstanding and non-progressive and the likelihood of further significant movement seems remote.

The property is located in a cul-de-sac of similar age and style properties off Chiswick High Road for local shops and amenities.

*Please delete as required

Subsidence, Heave or Landslip. Please report specifically on any evidence of subsidence, heave or landslip in the property or in the immediate vicinity.
There is no evidence of subsidence, heave or landslip

Valuation of property	Retention	Reinspection necessary: Yes/No*
£ 128,500	£Nil	No

Recommended insurance value. Main Property:	Recommended insurance value: Outbuildings	
£ 78,000 (maisonette only)	£	76 sq.m.

Appendix 4
Woolwich Cost of Moving Survey
(1996)

ENGLAND AND WALES

House Prices	Cost of Selling		Cost of Buying	
£25,000	Solicitor	£287	Solicitor	£296
	Estate Agent (sole agency)	£769	Land Registry	£40
			Searches	£86
			Stamp Duty	nil
			Home Purchase Report	£255
	TOTAL	**£1056**	**TOTAL**	**£677**
£50,000	Solicitor	£310	Solicitor	£319
	Estate Agent (sole agency)	£1039	Land Registry	£80
			Searches	£86
			Stamp Duty	nil
			Home Purchase Report	£255
	TOTAL	**£1349**	**TOTAL**	**£740**
£60,000	Solicitor	£323	Solicitor	£333
	Estate Agent (sole agency)	£1224	Land Registry	£100
			Searches	£86
			Stamp Duty	nil
			Home Purchase Report	£315
	TOTAL	**£1547**	**TOTAL**	**£834**
£80,000	Solicitor	£355	Solicitor	£372
	Estate Agent (sole agency)	£1609	Land Registry	£140
			Searches	£86
			Stamp Duty	£800
			Home Purchase Report	£330
	TOTAL	**£1964**	**TOTAL**	**£1728**
£100,000	Solicitor	£401	Solicitor	£421
	Estate Agent (sole agency)	£2009	Land Registry	£200
			Searches	£86
			Stamp Duty	£1000
			Home Purchase Report	£330
	TOTAL	**£2410**	**TOTAL**	**£2037**
£150,000	Solicitor	£465	Solicitor	£490
	Estate Agent (sole agency)	£2950	Land Registry	£230
			Searches	£86
			Stamp Duty	£1500
			Home Purchase Report	£380
	TOTAL	**£3415**	**TOTAL**	**£2686**
£200,000	Solicitor	£549	Solicitor	£585
	Estate Agent (sole agency)	£3859	Land Registry	£260
			Searches	£86
			Stamp Duty	£2000
			Home Purchase Report	£430
	TOTAL	**£4408**	**TOTAL**	**£3361**

Figures compiled by the University of Greenwich, School of Land and Construction Management

Reproduced by kind permission of Woolwich Building Society.

Index